Poverty has dire consequences on the ability to fulfil one's aspirations for life. Poverty has strong implications for social cohesion and societies' abilities to function in harmonious ways. This book presents the readers with the core concepts, latest development and knowledge about policies that work to eliminate absolute poverty.

This volume shows what the consequences are for the quality of life of those living in poverty. It describes life for people in poverty in general, but also deals more specifically with children, in-work poverty and the elderly, thus providing a life, generational and global perspective on poverty, including the impact on people's happiness levels. The book also discusses policies aimed at poverty reduction, such as changes to the labour market – including the risk of working poor – and shows that there is a variety of possible instruments available to reduce poverty. These range from direct provision of social security to ensuring education and a better functioning labour market.

Written in an engaging and accessible style, the book provides a succinct insight into the concept of *poverty*, how to measure it, the situation of poverty around the globe as well as different types of possible interventions to cope with poverty. Supporting theory with examples and case studies from a variety of contexts, suggestions for further reading, and a detailed glossary, this text is an essential read for anyone approaching the study of poverty for the first time.

Bent Greve is Professor of Welfare State Analysis in the Department of Society and Business at Roskilde University, Denmark. He has published widely on different topics surrounding the welfare state, including technology and the labour market, happiness and social policy, labour market policy, and most recently on populism and the welfare state. He is editor of *Social Policy and Administration*.

THE BASICS

The Basics is a highly successful series of accessible guidebooks which provide an overview of the fundamental principles of a subject area in a jargon-free and undaunting format.

Intended for students approaching a subject for the first time, the books both introduce the essentials of a subject and provide an ideal springboard for further study. With over 50 titles spanning subjects from artificial intelligence (AI) to women's studies, *The Basics* are an ideal starting point for students seeking to understand a subject area.

Each text comes with recommendations for further study and gradually introduces the complexities and nuances within a subject.

JAPAN
CHRISTOPHER P. HOOD

LANGUAGE (SECOND EDITION)
R.L. TRASK

MEN AND MASCULINITY
NIGEL EDLEY

MEDIA STUDIES (SECOND EDITION)
JULIAN MCDOUGALL AND CLAIRE POLLARD

MEDIEVAL LITERATURE
ANGELA JANE WEISL AND ANTHONY JOSEPH CUNDER

MODERNISM
LAURA WINKIEL

NARRATIVE
BRONWEN THOMAS

POETRY (THIRD EDITION)
JEFFREY WAINWRIGHT

POVERTY
BENT GREVE

THE QUR'AN (SECOND EDITION)
MASSIMO CAMPANINI

RESEARCH METHODS (SECOND EDITION)
NICHOLAS WALLIMAN

SEMIOTICS
DANIEL CHANDLER

SPECIAL EDUCATIONAL NEEDS AND DISABILITY (THIRD EDITION)
JANICE WEARMOUTH

SPORT MANAGEMENT
ROBERT WILSON AND MARK PIEKARZ

SPORTS COACHING
LAURA PURDY

TRANSLATION
JULIANE HOUSE

TOWN PLANNING
TONY HALL

WOMEN'S STUDIES (SECOND EDITION)
BONNIE G. SMITH

For a full list of titles in this series, please visit www.routledge.com/The-Basics/book-series/B

POVERTY

THE BASICS

BENT GREVE

Routledge
Taylor & Francis Group

LONDON AND NEW YORK

First published 2020
by Routledge
2 Park Square, Milton Park, Abingdon, Oxon OX14 4RN

and by Routledge
52 Vanderbilt Avenue, New York, NY 10017

Routledge is an imprint of the Taylor & Francis Group, an informa business

British Library Cataloguing-in-Publication Data
A catalogue record for this book is available from the British Library

Library of Congress Cataloging-in-Publication Data
Names: Greve, Bent, author.
Title: Poverty : the basics / Bent Greve.
Description: 1 Edition. | New York : Routledge, 2019. | Series: The basics | Includes bibliographical references and index.
Identifiers: LCCN 2019028289 (print) | LCCN 2019028290 (ebook) | ISBN 9780367276348 (hardback) | ISBN 9780367276362 (paperback) | ISBN 9780429297007 (ebook)
Subjects: LCSH: Poverty. | Poverty—Social aspects. | Economic policy. | Social justice.
Classification: LCC HC79.P6 G748 2019 (print) | LCC HC79.P6 (ebook) | DDC 339.4/6—dc23
LC record available at https://lccn.loc.gov/2019028289
LC ebook record available at https://lccn.loc.gov/2019028290

ISBN: 978-0-367-27634-8 (hbk)
ISBN: 978-0-367-27636-2 (pbk)
ISBN: 978-0-429-29700-7 (ebk)

Typeset in Bembo
by Apex CoVantage, LLC

CONTENTS

List of figures, tables and boxes   ix
Preface   xi
List of abbreviations   xiii

1   **Introduction**   1
    1.1   Why should we understand and have an
          interest in poverty?   1
    1.2   A snapshot of the situation   2
    1.3   Overview of the book   3
    1.4   A few delimitations   6
    1.5   A few concluding remarks   7
    References   8

2   **What is poverty and how can we measure it?**   9
    2.1   Introduction   9
    2.2   Absolute poverty   12
    2.3   Relative poverty   16
    2.4   Poverty as a multidimensional issue   21
    2.5   Relative position influences people's own position   27
    2.6   Inequality, justice and relation to poverty?   28
    2.7   Summing up   29
    References   30

3	**Reflections on the development in poverty and the situation around the globe**	**35**
	3.1 Introduction	35
	3.2 Development in the overall level of poverty	36
	3.3 Poverty development in affluent welfare states	37
	3.4 Poverty development in developing countries	43
	3.4.1 Africa	44
	3.4.2 Asia	44
	3.4.3 Latin America	47
	3.5 Summing-up what do we know?	48
	References	48
4	**Quality of life for those living in poverty**	**53**
	4.1 Introduction	53
	4.2 Cross-cutting issues related to a life in poverty	54
	4.3 Impact on children living in poverty	55
	4.4 In-work poverty a problem?	56
	4.5 Poverty in old age	60
	4.6 Happiness and poverty	62
	4.7 Summing-up – a generational perspective	63
	References	64
5	**Explanation of and possible policies aimed at reducing poverty**	**67**
	5.1 Introduction	67
	5.2 Why do we have poverty?	68
	5.3 Preventing poverty	70
	5.4 Instruments to cope with poverty	72
	5.4.1 Cash benefits and poverty	73
	5.4.2 In-kind benefits – services and poverty	75
	5.4.3 Financing and poverty	76
	5.4.4 Education	78
	5.4.5 Labour market policy	79
	5.4.6 Other instruments	80
	5.5 Target or not targeted benefits?	81
	5.6 Summing up	83
	References	83

6   International perspectives on poverty   **89**
   6.1 Introduction   89
   6.2 International organisations and poverty   90
   6.3 Migration and poverty   93
   6.4 Transfers from rich to poor countries   95
   6.5 Technology, economic development and poverty   98
   6.6 Summing up   98
   References   100

7   Concluding remarks   **101**
   7.1 Introduction   101
   7.2 Examples of successful poverty reduction cases   101
   7.3 Historical reasons for reduction in poverty   103
   7.4 Can we reach the UN goal?   104
   7.5 Conclusion   105
   References   105

   Index   107

FIGURES, TABLES AND BOXES

FIGURES

1.1 Development in absolute poverty since 1980 based
    on US$1.9 per day   3
2.1 Poverty gap in OECD countries in 2017   20
2.2 At risk of poverty or social exclusion by type of
    risk, EU-28, 2017   26
3.1 Poverty development in Europe   38
6.1 Net official development support as percentages of
    GDP in 2017   97

TABLES

2.1 Objective and subjective indicators related to
    having, loving and being   11
2.2 Absolute poverty in 2015, using US$1.9 per day
    (2011 prices)   15
2.3 At risk of poverty in the European Union, 2017   17
2.4 Number at persistent risk of poverty and
    depending on the threshold of median income in
    the European Union in 2017   18

2.5 Poverty rates in selected OECD countries 2014–2016   19
3.1 Poverty at the international poverty line of US$1.9
     per day (in 2011 PPP)   37
3.2 People at risk of poverty or social exclusion, by age
     group, 2016   40
4.1 At risk of in-work poverty within EU countries in
     selected years since 2010   59
4.2 The five most and least happy nations in 2019   63
5.1 Perceptions of underuse and overuse of benefits   82

BOXES

2.1 Central concepts   12
2.2 Poverty rates and poverty gap   19
2.3 Elements of multidimensional poverty   23

PREFACE

Poverty is still a daily life condition for many persons around the globe. It influences people's quality of life, it causes losses for societies and has an impact on social cohesion.

Despite this, in many ways there is still not agreement on how to measure and understand what poverty is. There is no common agreement of the causes of poverty, and there are different national and international understandings of what poverty can be considered to be.

However, at the same time it is important to know the core concepts, discussions and development with regard to poverty. This is the aim of this book, as it hopefully will enable readers to look into it from the many and very diverse angles. Therefore, the book includes conceptual elements, historical developments, regional differences and policies that might have an impact on poverty.

I would like to express my thanks to the contributors to my edited volume, the *Routledge International Handbook of Poverty*, and to those who reviewed the different chapters. This has helped me in the writing of this book.

Bent Greve,
May 2019

ABBREVIATIONS

CCT	Conditional cash transfers
DAC	Development Assistance Committee
ESSPROS	European System of integrated Social Protection Statistics
EU	European Union
GDP	Gross Domestic Product
ILO	International Labour Organization
IMF	International Monetary Fund
LIS	Luxembourg Income Study
MPI	Multidimensional Poverty Index
NGO	Non-governmental organisation
OECD	Organisation for Economic Co-operation and Development
PPP	Purchasing Power Parities
UN	United Nations
UNDP	United Nations Development Programme
WHO	World Health Organization

INTRODUCTION

1.1 WHY SHOULD WE UNDERSTAND AND HAVE AN INTEREST IN POVERTY?

Poverty has been on the agenda for many years and, given the UN goal of eradicating extreme poverty by 2030, it is central to understand the concepts used, the ways in which poverty can be measured and also to have an idea about why we see the development across the globe. The UN aim further being to reduce the absolute numbers living in poverty, not just the poverty rate. Poverty has dire consequences for individual persons, families, societies and, in fact, the development between countries and regions across the globe. If one wants to do something about poverty, it is also important to have an insight into what kind of instruments are available in order to cope with poverty. Thus, the aim of this book is to present the central concepts, the historical development in poverty and what we currently know about how to influence the level of poverty.

Thereby, a central focus throughout the book is how poverty relates to:

• different regions, including a number of especially large countries,
• various socioeconomic groups,

- different income levels,
- the life-cycle, and
- quality of life.

These are all key factors in understanding the consequences of the development in poverty around the globe today. However, it is not enough to know how many people are living in poverty. What it is like to be poor and to live in poverty can be used as a means for understanding the reasons for looking into different kinds of instruments that can change the situation; these are described and analysed in later chapters of the book. Thus, the consequences of living in poverty in relation to not only basic issues such as food, shelter and health, but also the impact on what is considered to be a good life, including well-being and happiness, are presented. Overall, this shows the reasons why poverty is an important topic and is the core of this first chapter. A few historical references as to when policies aimed at poverty were introduced are presented as part of indicating why this has been an important topic for a long time.

This chapter sets the scene for the book and explains why poverty, including the consequences of living in poverty, are important for an understanding of modern societies and their development. The first chapter is structured so that the next section presents a snapshot of poverty and its development across the globe, in order to understand the variations in, and the issues relating to, poverty in modern societies. A short overview is then given of what readers can expect in the following chapters, before a few delimitations are presented. Lastly, the chapter is concluded.

1.2 A SNAPSHOT OF THE SITUATION

This section shows the current situation of poverty across the globe, although it does not discuss how we can measure poverty, see instead, Chapter 2. The overall development is in many ways a success story. Many people have been lifted out of absolute poverty over the last 20–30 years. This is especially due to poverty reduction in two large countries, China and India, whereas there is still a strong issue and problems related to poverty when looking into the situation in the Sub-Saharan region (on this point, see Greve 2020 and Chapter 3 this volume).

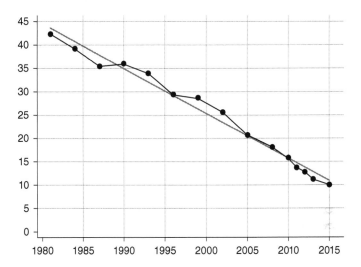

Figure 1.1 Development in absolute poverty since 1980 based on US$1.9 per day
Source: Based on World Bank data, see Hussain (2020).

Figure 1.1 shows the long-term development since 1980 in absolute poverty.

As the figure shows, there has been a strong decline, but – as presented later in the book – this does not mean that this has been the case globally. For developed countries, the book uses the relative poverty line as a core instrument to measure the development, as in the wealthier countries this is the one used in the main analysis of the development. Relative poverty has not been reduced to the same extent as absolute poverty, due among other things to the way in which it is measured. As shown later, monetary poverty is only one aspect of the information on the size and impact of poverty, including how it influences different groups. The numbers do further not inform about the causes, including the reasons for the decline.

1.3 OVERVIEW OF THE BOOK

Following this chapter, Chapter 2 presents and discusses how we can measure poverty. This is not only an academic exercise, but also an issue that is important if policy makers want to reduce the level of poverty. One needs to know how to measure it as this has implications for whether or not it has been eradicated, but also how it can vary in different places around the globe. The countries mainly in focus are the EU, North America, Australia, China and India, but regions around the globe are also included, given that when analysing absolute poverty, one needs to include, especially, Sub-Saharan Africa and Asia in the presentation.

The chapter includes a short depiction of the first studies in the UK on poverty in the early 20th century to set the scene for the concept of absolute poverty, which still today is an issue in relation to the understanding of global poverty. How and whether this can be used in all countries and how this might influence the perception of poverty in a variety of countries is included. After this, relative poverty is presented, which is an important way of understanding poverty in different countries, including its development and who is most at risk of living in poverty. From looking into poverty and the issue of deprivation, the chapter turns to the fact that poverty can be understood as a multidimensional issue. How society's provision of various types of services might influence the understanding of poverty is included, albeit part of this is covered in later chapters. Measurement issues to consider in the analysis also include the availability of data. The discussion of how best to measure poverty can be seen as an academic matter related to ensuring consistency in the knowledge hereof. However, the level at which the ceiling is set can have policy implications – a higher ceiling means that more people will be considered to live in or at risk of poverty. The chapter also reflects on the reasons why some people who are objectively wealthier than most people might experience the feeling of not being well off. In conclusion, the chapter presents the relationship between discussions on inequality and an understanding of what justice is.

After this more conceptual chapter, Chapter 3 tries to depict whether international goals, such as those of the UN, can be achieved. In doing so, it is important to look not only into the present situation, but also the historical development in different countries. Therefore, this chapter aims to give both a long time perspective on the development and a more detailed picture around the globe since the beginning of this century. As far as possible, the presentation is grouped into countries and uses welfare regimes clusters as an instrument to present the development. This helps in ensuring that, as far as possible, there is a similarity in living conditions as this could help in understanding whether it is the same type of development in all countries and whether differences/similarities can be found. These might reflect different ideological positions and understandings of how societies function, but also the choice in nation states of different policies aimed at poverty. The chapter tries to show trends in different countries related to who might live in poverty, including using a life-cycle approach, and thus includes a perspective of poverty from the cradle to the grave, albeit the principles related to this are covered in Chapter 4. The focus is mainly on developed countries; however, in order to use the concept of absolute poverty as well as presenting knowledge about where there has been a strong reduction in poverty, the chapter briefly includes developing countries. The regions to be compared on a global scale are mainly on continents, such as Africa, Asia, Europe, North America and Latin America.

It is, however, not sufficient to understand only the extent of poverty, but also to have an idea about what constitutes quality of life, and for those living in poverty, how to cope with it; this is the focus of Chapter 4. It attempts to describe life for people in poverty in general, but also deals specifically with children, in-work poverty and the elderly, thus including a life and generational perspective on the issue. At the same time, the chapter identifies those who are the most vulnerable groups in society.

Once the size and development of poverty and the quality of life are known, the next step, if one wants to eradicate poverty, is to find out what policy instruments are available. This is because there is not one individual policy that might help in eradicating poverty. This is the focus of Chapter 5. The chapter first presents a few typical explanations of poverty as a starting point for discussing policies aimed at poverty, such as economic growth (see also, however, Chapter 6) and changes in the labour market, including the risk of working poor. Social safety nets, education and the impact of types of taxes and duties are further elements that are presented, along with the existing evidence on a set of instruments that might reduce poverty. It also looks into why and how some policies, given the explanations of the reasons for poverty, can and have been used (this includes issues such as the level of welfare benefit and services, pensions, education, health and support to children in families).

Policies are not only about a national approach and international elements, such as international migration, for a variety of reasons are also touched upon, although the main part of this is covered by Chapter 6.

Therefore, Chapter 6 starts with a focus on the UN's goals of sustainable development and the goal of eradicating poverty. It presents the role of international organisations and collaboration in relation to poverty. This also includes a discussion on migration, transfers from rich to poor countries and international support for development mainly in less developed countries. Transfer of knowledge is seen as a further way of reducing poverty internationally. The relationship between poverty and technological developments, which might move production around the globe also from countries with an abundant number of workers and poverty, is discussed. Economic growth is touched upon, as it might be one way, but not the only one, of helping to alleviate poverty, although this will depend on the way in which economic growth is distributed. Recent rises in economic inequality indicates that it is also a question of how resources are distributed in different countries.

The final chapter concludes the book and tries to depict possible pathways with the aim of reducing or eradicating poverty. This includes a presentation of a number of successful cases around the world in reducing the number of people living in poverty. It also draws on historical reasons for reduction in poverty as an indicator of what can be done. This is supplemented by a discussion as to whether there is evidence and knowledge on which instruments are available for doing so. Lastly, it discusses the possible barriers to achieving the goals set by the UN.

1.4 A FEW DELIMITATIONS

There will always be delimitations in a book. This includes, due to the size of the book, the lack of detailed information on specific countries, even though references to the development in some countries are given. Very detailed presentations of regional issues are also limited, see instead Greve (2020), where more detailed presentations of the situation for all regions in the world can be found. In addition, many of the international organisations presented in Chapter 6 include detailed national information in their work and publications.

The book does not discuss the effectiveness of donations from richer to poorer countries. Instead, it makes the assumption that, as in other parts of societal development, one should be aware of how to get maximum value for money and how to avoid the unintended consequences of overspending. In this case, for example, that donations do not reduce the local ability to produce products and ensure economic and social development.

Overall, the focus is also on the role of the state as an actor able to alleviate poverty. This is not to neglect the fact that philanthropy might and does play a role in supporting development out of poverty both internally by country and internationally and also in the wake of, for example, specific crises. However, this is voluntary and not necessarily stable in its impact, so this will be touched upon only to a limited extent in the book. However, the role of the family and extended family is in several circumstances included in the analysis, as the internal distribution of resources can also influence who is actually living in poverty, albeit this is not always reflected in the statistics.

The book does not enter into a presentation and debate on how to evaluate anti-poverty programmes (see instead Barrientos and Villa 2015), but refers to the fact that evidence-based policies seem to be important in order to achieve the goals, given the resource constraints. It does, however, present a number of possible instruments to alleviate poverty.

Analysis and discussion of poverty can be highly complex when using mathematical models and approaches in the description. The aim of this book is to describe and explain and therefore, with only a few exceptions, it shows how to actually measure and calculate poverty, as well as giving explanations for change in, for the most part, a descriptive way.

1.5 A FEW CONCLUDING REMARKS

For reasons of justice and well-being, poverty is still an important topic. It is also a topic with strong positions and ideological perspectives on what is the best way to cope with it. The aim of this book is to present the current level of knowledge within the field as precisely as possible, so that readers can gain an idea about concepts, how poverty is defined and how it can be measured – including the strengths and weaknesses hereby. Furthermore, the book presents information on what we know about lives of those living in poverty and the consequences thereof, including how different instruments work in attempting to alleviate poverty and the consequences of using those instruments for people living in poverty.

Historically, poverty has imposed strong consequences within societies. This is still a risk, thus knowing about poverty can be an important aspect of how to develop societies in the best way.

REFERENCES

Barrientos, Armando and Juan Miguel Villa. 2015. 'Evaluating Antipoverty Transfer Programmes in Latin America and Sub-Saharan Africa. Better Policies? Better Politics?', *Journal of Globalization and Development* 6(1): 147–79.

Greve, Bent (ed.) 2020. *The Routledge International Handbook of Poverty*, 1st edn. Abingdon: Routledge.

Hussain, M. Azhar. 2020. 'Absolute Poverty', in Bent Greve (ed.), *The Routledge International Handbook of Poverty*, 1st edn. Oxon: Routledge.

WHAT IS POVERTY AND HOW CAN WE MEASURE IT?

2.1 INTRODUCTION

If policy makers want to reduce the level of poverty, they need to know how to measure it as this affects the results as to whether or not it has been reduced over time, or even eradicated, and it also indicates whether the instruments used have functioned correctly. They also need to know whether poverty can be different in various places around the globe, also given diverse circumstances in individual countries. The situation across the globe in different regions is presented and the countries mainly in focus are the EU, North America and Australia, whereas other countries are included in Chapter 3.

The chapter starts in section 2.2 with a short depiction of the first studies in the UK on poverty in the early 20th century, in order to set the scene for the discussion of the concept of absolute poverty, which is still an issue today in relation to the understanding of global poverty and the UN's goals. How and whether the concept of absolute poverty can be used in all countries, and how it might influence the perception of poverty in a variety of countries, is discussed. In the main part of the countries involved, it is more a question of the relative position for each individual. Therefore, in section 2.3 the concept of relative poverty is presented, which is an important way to understand poverty, especially in developed countries. There is also a discussion on issues related to whether, in fact, one is able to measure poverty and what one needs to be aware of when doing so. Lastly, this section includes a few data on its development.

However, some argue that looking into especially relative poverty is not sufficient as it mainly focuses on monetary aspects of poverty. There is instead a need, it is argued, to look into the issue of deprivation. This is done in section 2.4, which looks into how poverty can be understood as a multidimensional issue. This includes how society's provision of various types of services might influence the understanding of poverty, see also Chapter 4.

Measurement issues to consider in the analysis also include the availability of data for all three aspects. The discussion of how best to measure poverty can be seen as an academic matter related to ensuring consistency in the knowledge thereof. However, the level at which the ceiling is set can have policy implications. This is because a higher ceiling means that more people will be considered to be living in or being at risk of poverty. Section 2.5 reflects on the reasons why some people who are objectively richer than most people might experience the feeling of not being well off. Lastly, section 2.6 presents the relationship between discussions on inequality and the understanding of what justice is.

Data issues mean that in survey data the most vulnerable groups might not be reached (Gaisbauer, Schweiger and Sedmak 2019), which is not touched upon in detail here. This might cause an underestimation of the number, however, it is still the best available data and over time, even if is not fully precise, it is informative about the situation and development in regard to poverty.

Poverty can be seen as the lack of capabilities in order to be able to choose among a set of functionings in Sen's understanding (Hick 2012), or in Sen's words: 'the ability to take part in the life of society' (Sen 1999, 75). A definition of poverty can be broad or narrow: 'The narrowest definition concentrate on monetary income, which has the advantage of being relatively easily measurable. The broadest definitions see poverty as the denial of life chances to people' (Forder 1984, 303). Thus, the different concepts looked into

Table 2.1 Objective and subjective indicators related to having, loving and being

	Objective Indicators	*Subjective Indicators*
Having (Material and impersonal needs)	The level of living and environmental conditions	Subjective feelings of dissatisfaction/satisfaction with living conditions
Loving (social needs)	Relationships to other people	Unhappiness/happiness – feelings on social relations
Being (needs for personal growth)	People's relation to society and nature	Feelings of alienation/personal growth.

Source: Adapted from Allardt 1993, p. 93.

later in this chapter reflect the possible difference in definitions, but also that the focus on what poverty is can have implications for the understanding of the consequences hereof. The possible different definitions also point to the multidimensional issue of poverty, ranging from economic ways of interpreting it to how people are integrated and have options to be integrated in society's development.

The debate on poverty is also, in a way, related to the social indicator movement in the 1960s looking at having, loving and being. This can be seen in Table 2.1.

This is a clear focus in studies of poverty in order to ensure that not only monetary issues are part of the understanding of poverty, but also that life and the impact of poverty has a subjective dimension (cf. also later in the chapter on the position of relative poverty). 'Having' is often central in poverty studies, but there has been increased focus also on social needs and the options for social inclusion, as this can be difficult without the necessary economic means.

Here the focus is on how to understand the concept, but naturally a country's choice of poverty index can be influenced by whether to focus on the poorest in a society or whether to reduce the overall level of poverty (Kanbur et al. 2018).

The central concepts which are elaborated on in the chapter are shown in Box 2.1.

Box 2.1 Central concepts

Absolute poverty: The number of people having a daily income below a set level.

Relative poverty: The share of people having an equivalised income below a certain percentage of median income.

Persistent poverty: Households with an income below the poverty level in this year and at least two out of the three preceding years.

Material deprivation: The inability to afford a number of items considered necessary in a society.

Multidimensional poverty: The share of people influenced by several factors, e.g. not only income, but can also be health, education, housing etc.

2.2 ABSOLUTE POVERTY

There is no doubt that there have been people living in poverty throughout history. One of the first laws in relation to poverty was in England in 1388,[1] although not seen as very effective, it was an indication of the recognition of a problem. Poor laws in many countries followed over time and they later gradually developed into social assistance schemes. They were often concerned with beggars and how to contain them. They were also often related to harsh living conditions and a demand that people should work if they were able to. A distinction, as often seen in social policy, between deserving and undeserving was, at least indirectly, part of the discussion (Greve 2018). At the beginning, there was no clear definition of how to understand poverty. From early on, though, there have been indirect references to it, such as that there should be access to certain necessities for all in a society (Smith 1776).

The study by Rowntree is seen as the first study in the attempt to measure poverty. The study, undertaken in York in the UK in 1899, measured the required expenditure to buy 'the necessary nutrients at the lowest cost possible' (Rowntree 1901, 98), was seen as a way to identify who was living in poverty. This is sometimes also referred to as the necessary 'basket of goods' that needed to be available in order to survive and the money needed to buy it. Historically, this was mainly food, such as porridge. This also emphasises one of the issues with a level of absolute poverty, that what was necessary in 1899 is not the same as what one might argue as essential today. Therefore, the basket of goods needed might change over time. Using this approach can further be argued to be looking into basic needs, but not the wider ones required in order to be socially integrated in societies. It has even been argued that it was a relative line as it compared the standard of living of the poor with the rest of the population of York (Veit-Wilson 1986). Here, the use of the concept of necessary goods is seen as a good understanding of absolute poverty.

Still, having a discussion on what is necessary in order to survive is a first step to understanding the nature of poverty and then comes a debate on what in today's richer societies is important in order to avoid living in or at risk of poverty. The amount of money needed per day to avoid living in absolute poverty, as presented in the start of Chapter 1, might be different from country to country given that the cost of living varies across countries and also the availability of food can vary across countries. Given that there is inflation, the level will need to be updated from time to time to reflect the amount of money needed to survive. The absolute level of poverty is mainly used in developing countries (Ferreira et al. 2016).[2]

It also reflects different understandings of poverty, one related to standards of living and another related to minimum rights to resources (Atkinson 1989). Using income reflects a right to resources approach. Thereby it can also be important to know not only the number of people below a specified line, but also how far away from the line they actually are.

National ways of measuring absolute poverty can thus also be witnessed (e.g. for Mozambique, see Hussain 2020). However, if using a nationally defined basket of goods, it might be difficult to compare the level of poverty in different countries, which is also a reason for having set a line as a benchmark internationally for whether people are actually living in poverty. Ending poverty as we know it today also means that no one should have an income below the line set for absolute poverty.

As with other issues related to poverty, there are a number of measurement issues, which might also help in understanding why there is no consensus of how to set the line and how it is actually measured. One specific measurement problem, for example, relates to the fact that not all countries have solid information on income and also that there are differences in the estimated size of the hidden economy. This is because having an income from the hidden economy theoretically can mean that people are close to the chosen line (further statistical information on the development in the number of people around the globe living in absolute poverty is presented in Chapter 3).

Another criticism of using the absolute poverty line is that the main focus is on economic security, but not the wider aspects of personal security. Given that the poverty line can vary across countries and change over time, it does not by itself inform about what type of welfare states there are, or if there is even what we today consider a welfare state, or the possible impact of welfare states upon poverty (e.g. Saunders 2019). Furthermore, defining 'necessities' implies a normative judgement of what is important for different people (Saltkjel and Malmberg-Heimonen 2020).

There is also an issue about whether there is data available in order to make the measurement unambiguously. This includes information on income, as this is often collected through surveys. It also includes whether there is a hidden economy as this can have an impact and also the number of people living on a specific income. This makes it important to have an equivalence scale so that one is able to know whether the individual in a household has an income below the set poverty line. Typically, an equivalence scale is calculated by counting the first adult as 1, the second as 0.7 and each child as 0.5. This reflects the fact that there are economies of scale of more persons living together. Some persons might further have an income below the line in one year or have some assistance from family.

Another question, which is returned to in more detail in later chapters, refers to whether or not it is a short-term situation or whether it is a more persistent situation for the person and/or family in question. Thus, experiencing one year below an income poverty line due to starting up a company or studying might not mean the endurance of persistence of poverty over a longer time perspective. Some people with an income below the poverty line might also even be supported informally by the family (Daly 2018). This also refers to the historical debate about the possible cycle of poverty over the life course (Birnbaum et al. 2017).

Still, it is important to have a yardstick of how to define absolute poverty. It is today, in 2011 prices, $1.9 per day. It was updated to this level in 2015 by the World Bank based upon the poverty line in 15 of the poorest countries in the world[3] (see also Ferreira et al. 2016). Using this frame, there has been a decline in absolute poverty incidence around the globe from 42.3 per cent in 1981 to 10.0 per cent in 2015.[4] In 2015, the five countries with the highest number above this line (all above 70 per cent of the population) were: the Democratic Republic of Congo, South Sudan, Burundi, Madagascar and the Central African Republic. Thus, all countries from the continent of Africa, which is also the case for the 25 countries at the bottom of the list. Using the poverty line in the poorest countries reflects the fact that this better indicates what is necessary in order to avoid living in poverty in those countries. At the same time, this is also one of the reasons why other countries prefer to use a relative poverty line as this better reflects the actual position of different groups (see more in section 2.3). Using the same approach over time has the further advantage that even if data are not perfect, they will give an indicator of the movement in the number of people living in poverty.

Around the globe the level of absolute poverty varies considerably between regions, as shown in Table 2.2.

Table 2.2 Absolute poverty in 2015, using US$1.9 per day (2011 prices)

East Asia and Pacific	2,3
Europe and Central Asia	1,5
Latin America and the Caribbean	4,1
Middle East and North Africa	5,0
Other high Income	0,7
South Asia	12,4
Sub-Saharan Africa	41,1
World Total	10,0

Source: See note 4.

As can be witnessed from the table, the highest incidence of poverty is in Sub-Saharan Africa and this is also the region where the decline compared to others has been more limited. It is also above 10 percentage points in South Asia. This is because more people in South Asia have over time been lifted from poverty, even though this is still the region with the second highest number of people living in absolute poverty. So, overall, there has been a positive development, which is looked into in more detail in Chapter 3.

2.3 RELATIVE POVERTY

Absolute poverty, as defined in the previous section, focuses mainly on what, in reality, is needed to survive, for example basic necessities. The relative line, as the name indicates, focuses on the fact that persons in a society should not have an income below a certain line relative to what others in the same society have. It is therefore defined as being persons having an income below a percentage of an income. Typically, it is by now an income of certain percentage below the median income in a society. In the European Union (EU), it is typically calculated by using a threshold of 60 per cent of the median income, which is the income for exactly the person in the middle of the income distribution.

The reason for the calculation using the median income is to avoid the calculation being influenced by a few very high or very low incomes in a given society during the year in question.

A central issue is whether one year in relative poverty is a welfare problem and whether this can actually be described as a person living in poverty (who might be a student, a self-employed person, an artist), when in the next year that person might have an income above the poverty level. It could also be a retired person who has some wealth not accounted for in the income calculation and it could be a person who has a family and/or friends who support him. Therefore, within the EU it is often labelled as being 'at risk' of poverty, due to people's lifestyles being different and some people could have an individual feeling of living in poverty. As with absolute poverty, it can also be an issue of whether the income is for one person or a household and also, differences in purchasing power parities (PPP) can have an impact. The permanent risk of poverty is therefore often estimated using the current year and two out of the last three consecutive years of living in poverty.[5] Still, just one year might have detrimental effects.

Purchasing power parities should make it possible to compare across countries, but also have implications for where the line is set in different countries and further, that the survey used to estimate this calculation is based upon spending, not necessarily what those in poverty '*need to spend* in order to satisfy their needs' (Saunders 2018, 13).

This is also the case in relation to whether one should measure before or after social transfers, taxes and duties, because the welfare state's activities in fact cause redistribution so that the picture will be different if these activities are not included. There might also be an impact on whether the individual will have to buy, for example, health insurance and/or pay for a number of services ranging from day-care and education, to health- and long-term care. Thus, there can be a variety of consequences of the risk of living in poverty dependent on the way welfare states function.

Using relative poverty, Table 2.3 is an overview of different age groups and gender in the EU who are most at risk using the 60 per cent of median income as the threshold.

As can be seen from the table, in the EU, more than one in every five persons using the threshold of 60 per cent of the median income after social transfers are at risk of living in poverty. There is also a strong difference so that those most at risk are young women and, in general, women are more at risk than men. Children have a slightly higher risk than the elderly. There are large differences among the European countries, as there are across the world in the incidence of poverty.

Table 2.3 At risk of poverty in the European Union, 2017

	Total	Men	Women
All	22,4	21,6	23,3
< 16 years	24,4	24,4	24,5
16–24	29	28	30,1
25–54	21,5	21,1	21,9
>55	20,6	18,4	22,5
>75	19,9	15,7	22,9

Source: Eurostat, ilc_peps01, accessed 12 March 2019.

Table 2.4 Number at persistent risk of poverty and depending on the threshold of median income in the European Union in 2017

	Total	*Men*	*Women*
40%	3,1	3,1	3
50%	6,3	6,3	6,3
60%	11,3	10,8	11,6
70%	18	17	18,9

Source: https://ec.europa.eu/eurostat/data/database accessed 12 March 2019.

Using different limits gives a variation in the relative numbers, which is shown in Table 2.4.

The issue of one or more years in poverty is covered by analysing the risk of living persistent in poverty, which is defined as 'the percentage of the population whose equalised disposable income was below the "at-risk-of-poverty threshold" for the current year and at least 2 out of the preceding 3 years'.[6] This is used in Table 2.4. The table also indicates that the choice of threshold has a huge impact on the number of persons living at risk of poverty. In 2017, it is close to one in five if using the 70 per cent line, but only 3 per cent if using a 40 per cent threshold. The implication is that one needs to be aware of the choice of poverty line when discussing the possible size and impact of people living in poverty. Women also here have a higher risk than men.

The level around the globe is different. Table 2.5 shows the level in OECD countries which are not members of the EU for 2014–2016; more details and a discussion are presented in Chapter 3.

The table paints a picture of strong diversity in poverty rates, with the US, Israel and Turkey having the highest levels and Norway and Switzerland having the lowest levels. Thus, variation in the poverty level is an indication of differences in the policies aimed at to how to cope with poverty, as well as a possible variation in the way the labour market works.

Relative poverty can also be understood in a more subjective way, see section 2.5. There are both poverty rates and poverty gap, see definitions in Box 2.2.

The poverty rate does tell us something about the number who have an income below the set poverty line but does not inform us about how far from the line they are. This is the idea behind the poverty gap. In Figure 2.1 the poverty gap is shown for OECD countries in 2017.

Table 2.5 Poverty rates in selected OECD countries 2014–2016

Year	2014	2015	2016
Australia	0,128	..	0,121
Canada	0,126	0,142	0,124
Chile	..	0,161	..
Iceland	0,065	0,054	..
Israel	0,186	0,195	0,177
Japan	..	0,157	..
Korea	0,144	0,138	..
Mexico	0,167	..	..
New Zealand	0,109	..	..
Norway	0,081	0,081	0,082
Switzerland	0,099	0,091	..
Turkey	0,173	0,172	..
United States	0,175	0,168	0,178

Source: Available at OECD.Stat, www.data.oecd.org accessed 20 March 2019.

Note: The rate is different from the EU as it is 50 per cent of median income.

Box 2.2 Poverty rates and poverty gap

OECD definitions

Poverty rates: The poverty rate is the ratio of the number of people (in a given age group) whose income falls below the poverty line; taken as half the median household income of the total population. It is also available by broad age group: child poverty (0–17 years old), working-age poverty and elderly poverty (66-year-olds or more). However, two countries with the same poverty rates may differ in terms of the relative income level of the poor.

Poverty Gap: The poverty gap is the ratio by which the mean income of the poor falls below the poverty line. The poverty line is defined as half the median household income of the total population. The poverty gap helps refine the poverty rate by providing an indication of the poverty level in a country. This indicator is measured for the total population, as well as for people aged 18–65 years and people over 65.

Source: Available at https://data.oecd.org/inequality/poverty-gap.htm, accessed 10 April 2019.

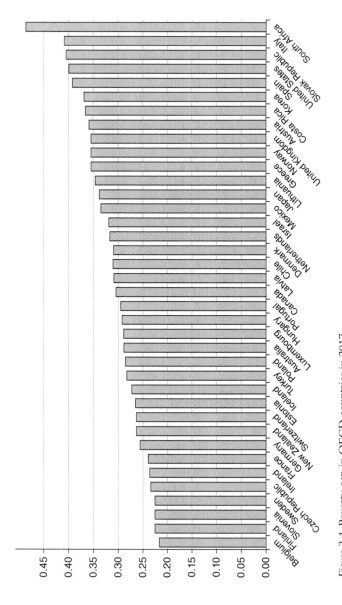

Figure 2.1 Poverty gap in OECD countries in 2017

Source: Available at https://data.oecd.org/inequality/poverty-gap.htm, accessed 10 April 2019.

The figure is a clear indication of that the distance to the relative poverty line is low in countries such as Belgium, Finland and Slovenia, but high in countries such as the Slovak Republic, Italy and South Africa. This means that, presumably, it will be more difficult to reduce the number in relative poverty in the latter three countries than in the former.

2.4 POVERTY AS A MULTIDIMENSIONAL ISSUE

Looking into monetary poverty might overlook other central aspects of daily life for people. Therefore, other approaches to understand poverty have been developed. This is also due to the fact that the development in a society looking at the macro level might mean that this overlooks those worst off, or as argued in the early days of the development of poverty as a multidimensional issue: 'this deprivational focus contrasts sharply with the conglomerate perspective, in which even a sharp regress in the conditions of the poor can be, quite possibly, outweighed by a suitable large surge in the fortunes of the affluent' (Anand and Sen 1997, 2). This is also the reason behind the development of a multidimensional poverty index (MPI).

A drawback of using money as the metric in the income-based measures also points out that the broader qualitative aspects of life are not included, these are elements such as housing, social inclusion, life expectancy, infant mortality, etc. Income-based measures might also mean that different groups are seen as living in poverty, than when using a broader metric, that is, including necessary goods. The elderly, for example, might have achieved necessities over their life time, which the young might not have. Thus, using deprivation as a measure can mean that young people are seen to a higher degree to be living in poverty than the elderly, when using a multidimensional approach rather than using only a monetary approach. This also points to the fact that one needs a variety of measures in order to paint a picture of who is living in poverty. In relation to housing, one needs to take into account whether the cost of accommodation is regulated or whether there is assistance to pay for it, see more in Chapter 5. It is, however, not only the cost of accommodation, but also the quality thereof, see also Box 2.3 on multidimensional poverty later.

The focus on living standards in a broader sense and, if possible, based on a consensus of what is necessary in order to live a decent life is part of the deprivation approach (Townsend 1979), including also having the amenities which are seen as customary in the country of residence. A weakness with this approach is that it can vary across countries making comparison difficult and what is customary also changes over time, dependent, for example, on technological development and the cost of new technologies. However, including a broader perspective is the reason behind the development of an MPI.

This MPI index focuses on health (nutrition, child mortality), education (years of schooling, school attendance), living standards (cooking fuel, sanitation, drinking water, electricity, housing, assets) (Alkire et al. 2016; Alkire and Jahan 2018), and with 1/3 weight for each of the three groups. Naturally, weighing can be discussed; however, if one wants to emphasise one dimension more than another, that is also possible. Thus, here the focus is not on income as the central parameter to understand and measure the development in poverty, it is based on the need to have reliable data, which are also comparable. The need for comparable data is also due to the fact that national definitions might vary and can be influenced by national priorities, including sometimes to make things look better than they actually are. Comparability also makes it possible to analyse and know about the development using the same indicators across countries.

The calculation of the MPI value is based upon incidence, for example, the numbers living in poverty. This is called the head-count ration (H). Further, the intensity which reflects the average share of indicator, as mentioned in the previous section, where poor people are deprived, which is labelled A. The MPI is then:

$$MPI = H \times A$$

This has a value between 0 and 1, the higher the value, the more people are living in multiple deprivation. Box 2.3 shows in more detail how the different elements of multidimensional poverty are defined, and the weight attached to each of them.

Naturally, there are data issues and problems collecting data, so they might not be precise enough to be argued to be the exact numbers, but still the indicators are a solid attempt to measure. Data

Box 2.3 Elements of multidimensional poverty

Health		Education		Living Standards					
Nutrition	*Child mortality*	*Years of schooling*	*School attendance*	*Cooking fuel*	*Sanitation*	*Drinking water*	*Electricity*	*Housing*	*Assets*
Any person under 70 years of age for whom there is nutritional information is under-nourished. 1/6	Any child has died in the family in the five-year period preceding the survey. 1/6	No household member aged 10 years or older has completed six years of schooling. 1/6	Any school-aged child+ is not attending school up to the age at which he/she would complete class 8. 1/6	A household cooks with dung, agricultural crop, shrubs, wood, charcoal or coal. 1/18	The household's sanitation facility is not improved (according to SDG guidelines) or it is improved but shared with other households. 1/18	The household does not have access to improved drinking water (according to SDG guidelines) or safe drinking water is at least a 30-minute walk from home, roundtrip. 1/18	The household has no electricity. 1/18	The household has inadequate housing: the floor is of natural materials or the roof or walls are of rudimentary materials. 1/18	The household does not own more than one of these assets: radio, TV, telephone, computer, animal cart, bicycle, motorbike, or refrigerator, and does not own a car or truck. 1/18

Source: Alkire and Jahan, 2018.

comes from 105 countries covering 5.7 billion people, close to 80 per cent of the population of the globe. Some are seen as vulnerable, defined as those who experience 20 per cent to 33.32 per cent of weighted deprivations, cf. Box 2.3, in severe poverty if it is above 50 per cent.

Using monetary poverty often implies the use of an equivalence scale, as argued earlier in the chapter. The choice hereof is difficult and this is even more difficult with regard to multidimensional poverty, due to the fact that households vary in size and composition and also vary over time (Alkire and Jahan 2018).

Based on the index as presented above, an overview of the global situation in 2018 is presented below:

> 1.3 billion people live in multidimensional poverty.
> 83% of all multidimensionally poor people in the world live in Sub-Saharan Africa and South Asia.
> Two-thirds of all MPI poor people live in middle-income countries.
> Half of the multidimensionally poor are children aged 0–17.
> 85% of MPI poor people live in rural areas.
> 46% of those who are multidimensionally poor live in severe poverty.
> In 2015/16, more than 364 million people are still MPI poor in India.
> In India, 271 million people moved out of poverty in ten years.
>
> (OPHI, 2018)[7]

This snapshot points in the same direction as the income-related data on poverty, see earlier in the chapter. Many of the 1.3 billion who live in multidimensional poverty are children; it is not only an issue in relatively poor countries, but also in middle-income countries. It also shows that children are at high risk, an issue to be returned to several times in the book. Still, the data also point to the fact that when looking into poverty, one needs to have a variety of ways of measuring and understanding both the actual and the historical development in poverty. According to this way of measuring poverty, the five countries with the highest MPI poor people around the globe are South Sudan, Niger, Chad, Burkina Faso and Somalia.

Poverty is thereby not only, as argued, an economic issue, but also relates to material deprivation. Another example of how this can be understood is the EU's definition of material deprivation related to not being able to pay for one or more of the following items:

1 to pay their rent, mortgage or utility bills;
2 to keep their home adequately warm;
3 to face unexpected expenses;
4 to eat meat or proteins regularly;
5 to go on holiday;
6 a television set;
7 a washing machine;
8 a car;
9 a telephone.[8]

(Eurostat Statistics Explained, 2018)

Material deprivation is defined as not being able to fulfil three of the numbered items, whereas the severe material deprivation rate is defined as not being able to pay for at least four. Naturally, one might discuss and have different opinions about how important all those items are; however, they indicate a set of goods that in modern, affluent societies can be important elements if one is not to, at least, feel socially excluded from the society's development. As can be seen, the elements included vary from those in the MPI index, reflecting that the options and possibilities vary strongly across the globe and in relation to the level of economic growth.

The EU has also combined three indicators (relative income poverty, material deprivation and household joblessness) as a multidimensional way to measure the development in poverty in the EU (Whelan, Nolan and Maître 2014). One reason is also that combining a few elements and presenting data hereabout makes it possible to monitor the development in many countries, including comparing the development.

In relation to understanding poverty, it is also an issue as to whether these aspects are overlapping. Figure 2.2 shows those at risk of poverty in the EU, having material deprivation and low work intensity and where they overlap.

The figure indicates that there are people who have both material deprivation and living at risk of poverty, which increases the

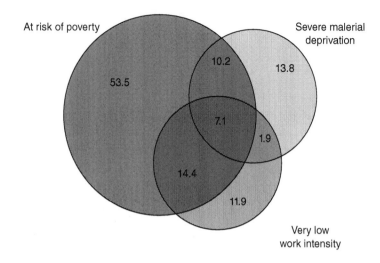

Figure 2.2 At risk of poverty or social exclusion by type of risk, EU-28, 2017

Source: Available at https://ec.europa.eu/eurostat/statistics-explained/index.php?title=File: People_AROPE_2019_1.png, accessed 20 March 2019.

risk of social exclusion in a given society. In 2017, there were 112.8 million people in the EU-28 who lived in households at risk of poverty or social exclusion. This is approximately one in every five within the EU. People at risk of poverty or social exclusion were in at least one of the following situations, as can be witnessed from the figure:

- at risk of poverty (60 of median income);
- severely materially deprived (e.g. four out of the nine items above); or
- living in households with a very low work intensity.

Social exclusion as a consequence of poverty is thus a strong issue even in the richer part of the world such as Europe. However, broadly, it explains that poverty besides the direct impact on the ability to live a decent life and buy the necessary nutrition can have broader impact on a person's life.

2.5 RELATIVE POSITION INFLUENCES PEOPLE'S OWN POSITION

One might feel poor even if one is not poor, in relation to the ceiling and calculation of relative poverty as described in section 2.3. This relates to that what one can describe as related to relative deprivation. This relates to two issues: one being the ability to live the life one wants, or aspires, to live; the other being the comparison with peers or others with whom individuals or families are making comparison. Thus, a poor person living with other poor persons does not necessarily have a higher subjective feeling of living in poverty than a more affluent person living close to other persons with higher incomes. The comparison can be both within a group and also across other groups (Runciman 1966).

It can also relate to how people perceive the degree of inequality in their country, so if people, for example, find that they live in a society with a very skewed income distribution, with few high income earners, a few in the middle and many at the bottom, the perception of social protection is lower than in countries where the situation is more equal and with a stronger social safety net (Ejrnæs 2020).

It is typically measured by asking people how their perception of their household's income is in relation to standard of living, including how difficult it is to live within their income. This ranges from whether it is comfortable, one can cope, it is difficult or very difficult.

Thus, poverty is not only an objective category, but is also influenced by the individual's perception hereof. However, at the same time, welfare state policies are mainly concerned with the policies that might change the more objective measures of poverty (Greve 2020). This points to the fact that there might be instruments available in order to cope with measured poverty, albeit not necessarily with perceived poverty; this is returned to later in the book.

People living in what can be labelled a poverty trap might be influenced to a stronger degree by their relative position. The poverty trap refers to the fact that even if getting a job or working more hours, the disposable income might not increase because, at the same time, higher income means higher income taxation and a reduction of in-cash and/or in-kind benefits. Thereby, people can have a feeling that they are deprived and that it is not possible for them to improve their life situation and live like those with whom they make comparison.

2.6 INEQUALITY, JUSTICE AND RELATION TO POVERTY?

The book does not focus in detail on inequality and measurement of that inequality for which, see instead, Cohen and Ladaique (2018); Caminada et al. (2019) and Atkinson (2015). Still, the existence of poverty is an indicator of inequalities in access to income and other options in societies. Those at the bottom of the income distribution have fewer options than those at the top and this is also the case with regard to the situation of those living in poverty – both in relation to absolute and relative poverty. Change in the level of inequality might thus reduce the level of poverty especially in times of economic growth and thus availability of greater resources for distribution. Thereby, change in inequality can also be an indicator informing about the development in poverty.

There is also a need to discuss whether the same income level will ensure the same standard of living for all, including having the capabilities to do what one wants. A question related to this is that there might be situations whereby 'a person with disability has special needs and thus requires more resources to escape a poor life' (Sen 1994, 334). One can further argue that 'Disability is therefore a particular form of the general phenomenon of capability-poverty' (Burchardt 2004, 746). This being an indicator that to avoid, in particular, material deprivation, it might be necessary to give specific treatment and/or redistribution to certain groups so that they have an opportunity to live the same kind of life as others, because although they might have an income above the poverty line, they might also have expenditures that mean there are material issues they are not able to fulfil.

It is more difficult to discuss whether a situation is just or unjust, because this implies normative viewpoints on how the situation ought to be. Still, the overall perception is that a high degree of inequality as well as poverty is not a just situation as it causes very different living conditions for persons and also causes the possibility of a negative impact on the way societies function (Stiglitz 2012;

Wilkinson and Pickett 2018; 2009). Thus, even if those having a lower income than the rest of society do not live in poverty, this might still have profound impact on the way societies actually work and function. This does not tell us precisely what to do and how much to redistribute, but is simply an indicator that just societies should try to do something in order to alleviate poverty, or at least try to reduce it as much as possible.

Recent years have seen an increase in the discussion of the proportion of income the most rich have, including the one per cent (see, for example, Piketty 2014). There seems, for example, to be a relation between an increase in income and wealth of the very rich and an increase in poverty (Kulkarni and Gaiha 2018). This is due, among other things, to an increase in the wealth of the rich which does not necessarily cause increased economic development and new jobs.

There is furthermore an issue about the democratic involvement of people in poverty. This includes both overall democratic participation but also how and whether they are actually involved in the decisions about their own life. This is because there are also power relations with regard to involvement and equality in access to influence can also be considered to be an issue in relation to poverty (Boone, Roets and Roose, n.d.). As shown in several studies, it is the case that participation is declining in line with lower levels of income and even if there is a lower limit below which participation does not fall, this is still an important issue (Ferragina, Tomlinson and Walker 2017). Participation includes elements of trust, neighbouring and political interest. This also reflects the fact that the issue of relative deprivation is more than having an income below a set level, but also causes overall less social integration in a society.

2.7 SUMMING UP

Poverty can be measured in a variety of ways – there is not just one way of doing it. Furthermore, the specific ways of doing it can have a variety of purposes. The specific way of defining the thresholds for living in or being at risk of living in poverty – whether absolute or relative – is up for discussion. Whether the threshold, for example, should be 50 per cent or 60 per cent of median income for relative poverty is not possible to give a definitive answer to. However, the choice of the percentage has an impact for how many people are counted as being at risk of living in poverty. Therefore, when looking into data, one first always needs to ask how they have been defined and also whether there has been a specific purpose of doing it in that way.

The analysis has also shown that monetary measures are not sufficient, that there is also a need to include different non-monetary elements in order to look into material deprivation.

The data we have indicates wide variety around the globe in the level of poverty, with the highest incidence in Sub-Saharan Africa, while at the same time there has been a decline around the globe in the number of people living in or at risk of poverty.

Measuring poverty does not inform about whether a society 'should' do something about it. This is, at the end of the day, a political and normative issue reflected in ideological issues. Still, a guideline might be the UN's goal to eradicate at least severe poverty, for example, the absolute poverty around the globe.

NOTES

1 See www.workhouses.org.uk/poorlaws/oldpoorlaw.shtml, accessed 9 March 2019.
2 *Journal of Economic Inequality* 14(2) is a special issue on global poverty lines.
3 See www.worldbank.org/en/topic/poverty/brief/global-poverty-line-faq, accessed 12 March 2019.
4 See http://iresearch.worldbank.org/PovcalNet/povDuplicateWB.aspx#, accessed 20 March 2019.
5 See https://ec.europa.eu/eurostat/statistics-explained/index.php?title=Glossary: Persistent_at-risk-of-poverty_rate, accessed 20 March 2019.
6 https://ec.europa.eu/eurostat/tgm/web/table/description.jsp, accessed 12 March 2019.
7 https://ophi.org.uk/multidimensional-poverty-index/global-mpi-2018/#t3, accessed 28 March 2019. On this webpage it is also possible to find other and more detailed data in different countries.
8 https://ec.europa.eu/eurostat/statistics-explained/index.php/Glossary: Material_deprivation, accessed 12 March 2019.

REFERENCES

Alkire, Sabina, Christoph Jindra, Gisela Robles and Ana Vaz. 2016. 'Multidimensional Poverty Index 2016: Brief Methodological Note and Results', *Global MPI 2016*. https://doi.org/10.1016/j.amc.2006.04.049.

Alkire, Sabina and Selim Jahan. 2018. 'The New Global MPI 2018: Aligning with the Sustainable Development Goals', OPHI Working Paper 121, University of Oxford.

Allardt, Erik 1993. 'Having, Loving, Being: An Alternative to the Swedish Model of Welfare Research' in Nussbaum, Martha and Amartya Sen (eds) 1993. *The Quality of Life*. Chicago: University of Chicago Press.

Anand, Sudhir and Amartya Sen. 1997. 'Concepts or Human Development and Poverty: A Multidimensional Perspective', in *Poverty and Human Development: Human Development Papers*. New York: United Nations Development Programme, pp. 1–20.

Atkinson, Tony. 1989. 'Poverty,' in John Eatwell, Murray Milgate and Peter Newmann (eds), *The New Palgrave Social Economics*, 2nd edn, Basingstoke: Palgrave Macmillan, pp. 204–14.

Atkinson, Tony 2015. 'What Can Be Done about Inequality?', *Juncture* 22(1): 32–41. https://doi.org/10.1111/j.2050-5876.2015.00834.x.

Birnbaum, Simon, Tommy Ferrarini, Kenneth Nelson and Joakim Palme. 2017. *The Generational Welfare Contract: Justice, Institutions and Outcomes*. Cheltenham: Edward Elgar Publishing.

Boone, Katrien, Griet Roets and Rudi Roose. 2019. 'Learning to Play Chess: How to Make Sense of a Politics of Representation with People in Poverty', *Social Policy & Administration* (in press).

Burchardt, Tania. 2004. 'Capabilities and Disability: The Capabilities Framework and the Social Model of Disability', *Disability & Society* 19(7): 735–51.

Caminada, Koen, Kees Goudswaard, Chen Wang and Jinxian Wang. 2019. 'Has the Redistributive Effect of Social Transfers and Taxes Changed over Time across Countries?', *International Social Security Review* 72(1): 3–31. https://doi.org/10.1111/issr.12193.

Cohen, Guillaume and Maxime Ladaique. 2018. 'Drivers of Growing Income Inequalities in OECD and European Countries', in Renato Miguel Carmo, Cédric Rio and Márton Medgyesi (eds), *Reducing Inequalities: A Challenge for the European Union?* Cham: Springer International Publishing. https://doi.org/10.1007/978-3-319-65006-7_3.

Daly, Mary. 2018. 'Towards a Theorization of the Relationship between Poverty and Family', *Social Policy & Administration* 52(3): 565–77.

Ejrnæs, Anders. 2020. 'Relative Deprivation and Subjective Social Position', in Bent Greve (ed.), *The Routledge International Handbook of Poverty*, 1st edn. Abingdon: Routledge.

Ferragina, Emanuele, Mark Tomlinson and Robert Walker. 2017. 'Poverty and Participation in Twenty-First Century Multicultural Britain', *Social Policy and Society* 16(4): 535–59.

Ferreira, Francisco H.G., Shaohua Chen, Andrew Dabalen, Yuri Dikhanov, Nada Hamadeh, Dean Jolliffe, Ambar Narayan, et al. 2016. 'A Global Count of the Extreme Poor in 2012: Data Issues, Methodology and Initial Results', *The Journal of Economic Inequality* 14(2): 141–72. https://doi.org/10.1007/s10888-016-9326-6.

Forder, Anthony. 1984. *Theories of Welfare*. London: Routledge Kegan Paul.

Gaisbauer, Helmut, Gottfried Schweiger and Clemens Sedmak. 2019. *Absolute Poverty in Europe*. Bristol: Policy Press.

Greve, Bent. 2018. *Social and Labour Market Policy: The Basics. Social and Labour Market Policy: The Basics*. https://doi.org/10.4324/9781315150802.

Greve, Bent. (ed.) 2020. *The Routledge International Handbook of Poverty*, 1st edn. Abingdon: Routledge.

Hick, Rod. 2012. 'The Capability Approach: Insights for a New Poverty Focus', *Journal of Social Policy* 41(2): 291–308. https://doi.org/10.1017/S0047279411000845.

Hussain, M. Azhar. 2020. 'Absolute Poverty', in Bent Greve (ed.), *The Routledge International Handbook of Poverty*, 1st edn. Abingdon: Routledge.

Kanbur, Ravi, Tuuli Paukkeri, Jukka Pirttilä and Matti Tuomala. 2018. 'Optimal Taxation and Public Provision for Poverty Reduction', *International Tax and Public Finance*. https://doi.org/10.1007/s10797-017-9443-6.

Kulkarni, Varsha S. and Raghav Gaiha. 2018. 'Beyond Piketty: A New Perspective on Poverty and Inequality in India', GDI Working Paper 2018–033. Manchester: The University of Manchester.

Piketty, Thomas 2014. *Capital in the Twenty-First Century*. Cambridge, MA: Harvard University Press.

Rowntree, B. Seebohm. 1901. *Poverty: A Study of Town Life*. London: Macmillan.

Runciman, Walter Garrison. 1966. *Relative Deprivation & Social Justice: A Study of Attitudes to Social Inequality in 20th Century England*. Berkeley, CA: University of California Press.

Saltkjel, Therese and Ira Malmberg-Heimonen. 2020. 'Absolute or Relative? Definitions and the Different Understandings of Poverty', in Bent Greve (ed.), *The Routledge International Handbook of Poverty*, 1st edn. Abingdon: Routledge.

Saunders, Peter. 2019. 'Poverty', in Bent Greve (ed.), *The Routledge International Handbook of Poverty*, 1st edn. Abingdon: Routledge.

Saunders, Peter. 2018. 'Monitoring and Addressing Global Poverty: A New Approach and Implications for Australia', *The Economic and Labour Relations Review* 29(1): 9–23.

Sen, Amartya. 1999. *Development as Freedom*. Oxford: Oxford University Press.

Sen, Amartya. 1994. 'Well-Being, Capability and Public Policy', *Giornale Degli Economisti e Annali Di Economia*, July/September: 333–47.

Smith, Adam. 1776. *An Inquiry into the Wealth of Nations*. Available at https://doi.org/10.7208/chicago/9780226763750.001.0001.

Stiglitz, Joseph E. 2012. *The Price of Inequality: How Today's Divided Society Endangers Our Future*. New York: W.W. Norton & Company.

Townsend, Peter. 1979. 'Introduction: Concepts of Poverty and Deprivation', *Poverty in the United Kingdom: A Survey of Household Resources and Standards of Living*. London: Allen Lane.

Veit-Wilson, John H. 1986. 'Paradigms of Poverty: A Rehabilitation of B.S. Rowntree', *Journal of Social Policy* 15(1): 69–99.

Whelan, Christopher T., Brian Nolan and Bertrand Maître. 2014. 'Multidimensional Poverty Measurement in Europe: An Application of the Adjusted Headcount Approach', *Journal of European Social Policy* 24(2): 183–97. https://doi.org/10.1177/0958928713517914.

Wilkinson, Richard and Pickett, Kate. 2009. *The Spirit Level – Why Equality Is Better for Everyone*. London: Allen Lane.

REFLECTIONS ON THE DEVELOPMENT IN POVERTY AND THE SITUATION AROUND THE GLOBE

3.1 INTRODUCTION

In order to find out whether international goals of reducing poverty, as presented in Chapter 1, are achieved, it is important to look into not only the present situation, but also at historical development. Therefore, the aim of this chapter is to give both a long-term perspective on the development and in section 3.2, a more detailed picture of change around the globe, mainly since the beginning of this century. Overall, the chapter tries to show trends, in different countries, related to who might live in poverty, including using a life-cycle approach and thus include a poverty perspective from the cradle to the grave, which is used in the various subsections, especially related to which age groups are at risk.

As far as possible, the presentation is grouped into regions and of countries within them. In relation to the EU, welfare regimes clusters are used as an instrument to present development as a way of depicting whether different welfare states can have variations in what the situation is like, (see further in section 3.3). This approach helps to achieve, as far as possible, similarity in context and conditions, as this may help us to understand whether it is the same type of development in all countries and whether differences/similarities can be found. These might reflect different ideological stances and understanding of how societies function, but also different policies aimed at poverty, which are presented in more detail in Chapter 5.

The focus is mainly on developed countries; however, in order to use the concept of absolute poverty as well as presenting knowledge about where there has been a strong reduction in poverty, the chapter briefly includes developing countries. The regions to be compared on a global scale are mainly on continents, such as Africa, Asia, Europe, North America and Latin America.

3.2 DEVELOPMENT IN THE OVERALL LEVEL OF POVERTY

Looking at it from a long, historical perspective, since the beginning of the 19th century there has been a remarkable reduction in absolute poverty and an even faster decline since the 1950s (Jefferson 2020). There are a number of reasons for the decline, which are returned to later.

There are many and varied ways into poverty, including family breakdown, educational failure, personal debt, addiction and unemployment (Pantazis 2016), and it can further be due to climate impact, civil war, military conflict, etc. Thus, development is always influenced by a wide variety of factors, which naturally also means that even a snapshot of the development does not shed light on the causes, which can vary from country to country, and from one year to the next, so there might be individual as well as collective reasons. Still, it is useful to have an overview of recent developments.

Table 3.1 presents a snapshot of the overall development from 2013 to 2015 in absolute poverty.

The good news is that there has been a decline in the number of people living in absolute poverty and this has, in fact, fallen by around 70 million people from 2013 to 2015. At the same time, the table also shows that more than 400 million people – and an increasing absolute number in Sub-Saharan Africa – still live in absolute poverty using the scale of US$1.9 per day in 2011 prices. Looking at the head-count ratio, it varies from 1.5 per cent in Europe and Central Asia to more than 40 per cent in Africa. Despite the growing absolute numbers, there has been a relative decline from 42.5 per cent to 41.1 per cent from 2013 to 2015. The world is thus still far from achieving

Table 3.1 Poverty at the international poverty line of US$1.9 per day (in 2011 PPP)

Region	Headcount ratio (%)		No. poor (millions)	
	2013	2015	2013	2015
East Asia and Pacific	3.6	2.3	73.1	47.2
Europe and Central Asia	1.6	1.5	7.7	7.1
Latin America and the Caribbean	4.6	4.1	28.0	25.9
Middle East and North Africa	2.6	5.0	9.5	18.6
South Asia	16.2	12.4	274.5	216.4
Sub-Saharan Africa	42.5	41.1	405.1	413.3
World Total	**11.2**	**10.0**	**804.2**	**735.9**

Source: Available at www.worldbank.org/en/news/press-release/2018/09/19/decline-of-global-extreme-poverty-continues-but-has-slowed-world-bank, accessed 12 March 2019.

both the abolition of poverty and reaching the UN goal of eradicating extreme poverty by 2030.

Looking further back, there has been an even stronger decline in the number of people living in absolute poverty, especially as a consequence of the growing economic prosperity in South Asia, and where, also from 2013 to 2015, the main decline in the numbers living in absolute poverty has taken place. Economic growth in China and India, especially, has contributed towards this.

3.3 POVERTY DEVELOPMENT IN AFFLUENT WELFARE STATES

This section focuses on development in the more affluent welfare states and therefore, in contrast to the more developing countries using a relative approach. It is split into Europe, North America and Australia.

The overall development is, as depicted in Chapter 2 and Table 3.1, that there has been a decline in absolute poverty, albeit already for some time at a low level. However, as discussed in Chapter 2, in more affluent countries it might be more important to look into relative poverty as this illustrates the position in societies and the risk of social exclusion. Here the picture is more diverse with higher levels in the US than in Europe.

The overall picture of the EU is highlighted in Chapter 2, however, the development is not presented, this is seen in Figure 3.1,

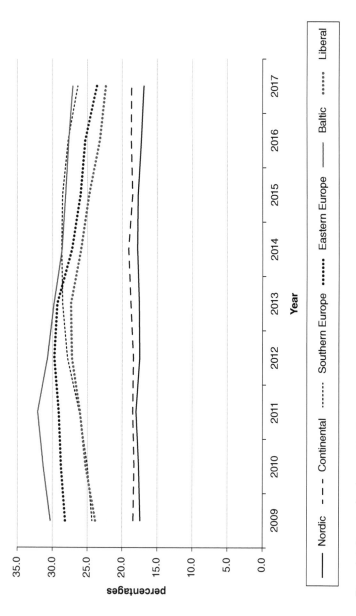

Figure 3.1 Poverty development in Europe

Source: Own calculations based upon Eurostat [ilc_peps01].

using the 60 per cent of median income as the benchmark and with countries split into the classical welfare regimes (Nordic, Continental, Liberal) and supplemented with Southern Europe, Eastern Europe and the Baltic countries. This is apparent despite the fact that, naturally, there are differences in national policies with regard to poverty reduction.

The figure shows that poverty is the lowest in the Nordic and Continental countries, i.e. the Western and Northern parts of Europe. The development has been stable from 2009 to 2017. In the Southern and Eastern European countries there was an increase after the financial crisis, which has been redressed except in Southern Europe where the poverty level in 2017 was higher than it was in previous years. Even in the liberal regime (Ireland and the UK), there has been a slight decline in the number of people at risk of living in poverty.

So, using welfare regime as a structuring device illustrates differences in levels, but also that there are different options in welfare states for reducing the level of poverty; although, see more in Chapter 4, which shows that market forces, especially the labour market, influence the number of people living in relative poverty. It seems that there is a clear connection between public sector spending on social policy and the level of poverty as the Nordic and Continental regimes spend more and have lower levels. It is not a full explanation given that the spending level is very low in the Baltic and Liberal countries, but higher in Southern and Eastern European countries. This thereby indicates that the classical discussion on level of spending, who gets benefits and poverty are still related (Brady and Bostic 2015; Korpi and Palme 1998).

Given the rise in recent years of inequalities in many countries in Europe, this also shows that the welfare states, in fact, have been able to lift more people out of poverty than in previous years, which is also shown in a long-term perspective using LIS data (Caminada et al. 2019).

A question in Europe, as elsewhere, is who is most at risk of living in poverty? This is shown in Table 3.2 for different age groups.

Children are, on average, the group most at risk of living in poverty, although not in all countries. In Baltic countries it is, for example, older people and in Denmark, Germany and the Netherlands,

Table 3.2 People at risk of poverty or social exclusion, by age group, 2016 (% of specified population)

	Total	Children (aged 0–17 years)	Adults (aged 18–64 years)	Older people (65 years and over)
EU-28	23,5	26,4	24,2	18,2
Belgium	20,7	21,6	21,7	16,4
Bulgaria	40,4	45,6	37,2	45,9
Czech Republic	13,3	17,4	13,0	10,1
Denmark	16,7	13,8	20,2	9,2
Germany	19,7	19,3	20,2	18,3
Estonia	24,4	21,2	20,3	41,4
Ireland	24,2	27,3	24,4	17,4
Greece	35,6	37,5	39,7	22,0
Spain	27,9	32,9	30,4	14,4
France	18,2	22,6	19,2	10,0
Croatia	27,9	26,6	26,9	32,8
Italy	30,0	33,2	31,5	23,2
Cyprus	27,7	29,6	28,1	22,9
Latvia	28,5	24,7	25,0	43,1
Lithuania	30,1	32,4	27,3	37,4
Luxembourg	19,8	22,7	21,0	9,1
Hungary	26,3	33,6	27,2	15,1
Malta	20,1	24,0	17,3	26,1
Netherlands	16,7	17,6	18,4	10,0
Austria	18,0	20,0	18,6	13,7
Poland	21,9	24,2	22,7	16,1
Portugal	25,1	27,0	25,6	21,8
Romania	38,8	49,2	37,0	34,0
Slovenia	18,4	14,9	19,1	19,9
Slovakia	18,1	24,4	17,6	12,3
Finland	16,6	14,7	18,2	13,6
Sweden	18,3	19,9	18,1	17,0
United Kingdom	22,2	27,2	21,8	18,0

Source: https://ec.europa.eu/eurostat/data/database, ilc_peps01, accessed the 28th of March, 2019.

adults aged 18–64. At the same time, in-work poverty has been an important factor in many countries, including in the Baltic countries (Aidukaite and Hort 2019). This is another indicator that national policies also have an impact on who is most at risk. Overall, if looking at it from level of education, those without education have the highest risk, most likely due to weaker attachment to the labour market.

Not all are positive about the development, arguing that it has been a disappointing development especially among children and those in the working age group (Goedemé, Hills and Cantillon 2019). This is partly a reflection of the diverse development across European countries and that the ambition of what is labelled a decent income has declined and that the development in policies aimed at the reduction of poverty has been reduced.

In North America there is also a high and persistently high level of poverty from around 10 per cent in Canada, 15 per cent in the US and more than 40 per cent in Mexico. There has in the long-run been a decline in the level of poverty, but it has increased in recent years and there are only limited developed welfare systems to help in alleviating the consequences of poverty in those countries, naturally with some variations (Kane 2020). There is evidence that the low level of benefits, also since the 1996 welfare reform, has had a negative impact on poverty, the argument being that this is due to a neoliberal development in the US, 'in which market forces are prioritized over government regulation and private responsibility is celebrated over collective processes' (Kane 2018), and also including a perception that those living in poverty have brought it on themselves.

In 2017, the poverty rate in the US using the national measurement was above 12 per cent, with the lowest rates among White, non-Hispanic, higher for women than for men, higher for non-US citizens, those not having a job and people with disabilities (Fontenot, Semega and Kollar 2018). In the US, it has become more difficult to move out of poverty, witnessed by the fact that 43 per cent of children born in poverty will continue to live in it for the rest of their lives (Reich 2015). Thus, despite the fact that child poverty has been reduced over the last 30–40 years, mainly due to safety nets developed, the level is still high. However, there are still strong differences, so that 'poverty among Black non-Hispanic and Hispanic young children is more than twice that among White non-Hispanic young children' (Pac et al. 2017).

In the US, there has been a stronger focus on in-kind benefits in recent years (see more on the difference between in-kind and in-cash benefits in Chapter 5). The impact of various instruments is also shown by the fact that from 2008 to 2017 universal health insurance could have reduced the incidence of multidimensional poverty by around 17 per cent and that increases in incomes for the young and the elderly would have the highest possible impact in reducing multidimensional poverty (White and Bailleuel 2020).

In Australia and New Zealand, as in other countries, there are people living in poverty. The long-term trend has been one of reduced poverty. Perhaps surprisingly in an affluent country, it is also possible to witness absolute poverty using the scale of $1.9 per day, showing that 0.59 per cent of the population has an income below this line; if removing the self-employed, the figure is 0.14 per cent (2011–2012 data) (Saunders 2018). In Australia, it is problematical to use a relative poverty line given the strong means-testing of social benefits, as this results in, when using equivalised income, which is very sensitive to where the line is positioned, a risk of over or underestimation (Saunders and Naidoo 2018).

Further, in Australia, it is clear that using different approaches yields different information. Using the incidence of multiple deprivation, i.e. the lack of a number of what are agreed to be essential items, gives a different profile of who is living poverty compared to using the poverty rate. Using a poverty rate of 50 per cent of median income shows that close to one out of four aged 65+ are living in poverty, whereas using a multiple deprivation lacking two items (and, in fact, also with one and three) shows that the age group of 15–24 has the highest incidence, which with two items is 14.9 per cent (data collected 2014/2015). Otherwise, the picture is the same as in other countries of those outside the labour force and unemployed having a higher risk than those employed full-time and part-time (Saunders and Naidoo 2018, Table 2, 342).

In general, one can argue that the development in poverty in more affluent welfare states is highly contingent on the size of that welfare state, including the size of, and the access to, a number of welfare benefits (Dewilde 2020), see also more on benefits and services in Chapter 5.

Looking into the development within the OECD, as it covers the most affluent countries, the overall problem is that 'in many OECD countries the bottom 20 per cent, hence poor households (based on a relative poverty criterion) have been the primary losers from the decline in redistribution' (Causa and Hermansen 2017, 44). Changes in policies have thus not had the same impact on all. Young people seem to have been harder hit (Erk 2017), including also that unemployment has been high for young people. This also as those at the bottom of the income distribution, at least in Southern Europe, but presumably also many other places, are now younger than those in the same position before the crisis (Matsaganis and Leventi 2014). As mentioned earlier, there are a number of possible reasons for ending up in poverty, including family breakdown, educational failure, personal debt, addiction and unemployment. This is an indicator that a variety of instruments might be necessary in order to cope with poverty and that this might vary from country to country, see more on instruments in Chapter 4.

Challenges with regard to poverty in the years to come revolve around a classical issue of the labour market situation, including whether non-standard employment means a higher risk of working poor, see also Chapter 5. The demographic trends towards more people outside the labour market can also cause difficulties in ensuring low levels of poverty (Summers 2020), although the elderly are not living in poverty in all affluent countries.

3.4 POVERTY DEVELOPMENT IN DEVELOPING COUNTRIES

This section looks into the main regions of the world and is therefore split into several subsections. It starts with Africa, being the region in the world with the largest number of people living in absolute poverty, as shown in Chapter 2. It is a crude division and, naturally, in the different regions some countries fare better than others; still, this split into different regions has been necessary in order to give an overview of the development. In order to elicit more detailed information on individual countries' development, one can use the many data that are available from a number of international organisations, such as the World Bank, UNICEF, etc., see more in Chapter 6.

In general, it looks like the different ways of measuring poverty give more or less the same results and, further, the size and comprehensiveness of social protection influence the level of poverty (Wagle 2020).

3.4.1 AFRICA

For some time, but this has not always been the case, Africa has been the place with the Sub-Saharan region as the area in the world with the highest level of absolute poverty, see Table 3.1; a continent and region which, due also to demographic reasons despite a decline in the proportion of the population below the poverty line, has an increase in absolute numbers above the line. As in other continents, there are huge variations across the countries reflecting different histories and possibilities for economic development.

Several reasons are behind this development. This includes a persistently high fertility rate where productivity in society is not able to increase production sufficiently to help in ensuring that there is no increase in the number of people in absolute poverty. It is also a continent with a large degree of inequality where, in principle, increased redistribution should make it possible to reduce the number of people living in poverty. Options and possibilities due to geographical and climate change also have an impact on the development as more land is not fertile, or at least not fertile enough to help in the reduction of the number of people living in poverty.

Many years of instability and civil war have also had an influence – there have been difficulties in developing production and also that part of societies' resources is spent on non-welfare enhancement issues. Lack of stability and transparency also influence the ability to be able to cope with poverty. An increase in economic growth and reduced fertility together with redistribution might help in reducing poverty, but this might take some time.

3.4.2 ASIA

In Asia, poverty reduction has been strong in many countries over the last 25–30 years, so that fewer people today are living in absolute poverty compared to previous years. This has especially been the case in China and India.

In Asia, the reduction in poverty has mainly been due to strong economic growth in several of the countries, but the impact of the use of cash transfers can also be witnessed (Bastagli et al., 2018).

A specific issue is the development in rural poverty, as economic development has often taken place mainly in the major cities and thus those living in rural areas continue to live in poverty to a larger degree. However, it seems that, if feasible, a strategy of increasing commercialisation and also a higher diversity of production might be a possible way to reduce poverty (Imai, Gaiha and Bresciani 2020). This also emphasises that the transition and how it is carried out in different types of production can be an important issue in relation to the reduction of poverty.

In China, there is a minimum livelihood guarantee called the Dibao system, in which regional limits are set for what is necessary and which is aimed at those sections of the population with lower incomes. In a way, one can argue that these different thresholds are another way to depict and describe what is necessary to avoid living in absolute poverty. This can, as well as the economic growth in China, help to explain the strong decline in the number of people living in poverty (Alkire and Shen 2017), which also shows the regional differences in the numbers in poverty and that rural areas, as in many other countries, often have a higher level of poverty than what is seen in the cities. This shows that there is also a strong variation of who is living in poverty if using an income measure or the multidimensionality measure.

The high level of rural poverty is despite the fact that since the 1980s more than 700 million rural Chinese are no longer living in poverty, which also means that the incidence of poverty has changed from 75 per cent in 1988 to 10 per cent in 2013 (Chuliang, Shi and Sicular 2018). This also shows that economic growth has been part of the story, but also that increased inequality at times has increased the problem.

This further raises the issue of whether one should try what has been done in China: to make poverty alleviation resettlement, e.g. by supporting voluntary and/or obligatory relocation of persons from one area to another with better prospects. However, this has both positive and negative connotations which are influenced by whether or not the resettlement is voluntary or forced and under what conditions the resettlement takes place. Thus, for example, it seems to be more positive for the young generation, who are more willing to resettle voluntarily (Xue, Wang and Rogers 2020).

Rural poverty is a strong issue in many Asian countries, and this is also the case in India. There has been a strong reduction in the level of poverty, as in China, over the last 50–60 years, with a large difference between the rural areas and the cities (25 per cent in rural and 15 per cent in cities in 2012–2013). As in other countries, there are wide regional variations in the level of poverty, ranging from provinces with 40 per cent to around 1 per cent in 2012. This while at the same time there has been an increase in the number of millionaires, who are expected to number 372,000 in 2022. This shows a country with a very diverse and widespread poverty, even if the economic development has been positive with regard to the ability to reduce the level of poverty (Kulkarni and Gaiha 2018). One issue, not often reported in the analysis of poverty, is that part of the population despite being above the poverty line, are 'at risk of deprivation in the face of disasters and economic shocks' (Narayan and Murgai 2016, 3), which also shows that vulnerability is still high in India. This seems to be in contrast to the development in Vietnam, which is also a country where poverty has declined rapidly.

There has been a discussion as to whether higher income in the cities also would cause better living standards in the countryside. This seems, at least over the long-run, to have been the case in India (Datt, Ravallion and Murgai 2016).

In most of Asia, there has been a strong decline in the level of poverty, although it has still not been eradicated. Japan, for example, has a low level of absolute poverty, but still has, see Table 2.5, close to one in six people living in relative poverty, despite also being a country with a high degree of economic equality. There are still, especially in the countryside, many people living in poverty and in living conditions with a high degree of deprivation. Economic growth is seemingly one of the main reasons for this development, albeit one needs to be aware that this does not always mean a lower level if the growth is distributed unequally.

3.4.3 LATIN AMERICA

The continent of Latin America had around 25 million people in 2015 living in absolute poverty (see Table 3.1). It is a continent with a wide variety across countries of the risk of living in poverty. The lowest rates are in Uruguay and Chile and the highest in Honduras and El Salvador.

Latin America is also the continent where conditional cash transfer programmes (CCT) emerged in the 1990s and where most countries by now have one or another kind of social assistance, reaching almost one in every five (around 130 million people) in 2016 (Arza and Maurizion 2020). In 1998, only Mexico and Brazil had a CCT programme, whereas in 2018 all countries in the region with the exception of Cuba and Venezuela had those programmes (Cruz-Martínez 2019). Part of the reason for the strong development in these programmes is argued to be the support in the form of technical assistance and loans from the World Bank. The conditions attached to receiving these benefits include that children must attend school and must also get the necessary vaccinations, etc. They were argued as a way of ensuring education for children and making it possible to increase the likelihood of getting an education, but were also intended to help improve health, for example, by obligations to participate in vaccination programmes.

However, not all studies show that the results have been achieved, except for the fact that those receiving the benefit have a better livelihood than they would otherwise have. It has further been argued that it reduces the incentive for some people to take up a job as there is income, while on the other hand it makes it possible for others to take a job as they now have money to pay for transport. Overall, it is argued that there is not a significant negative impact on incentives (Arza and Maurizion 2020).

Even if the short-term outcome of the programme seems positive overall, there is still only limited knowledge about whether it will achieve its long-term goals of changing the intergenerational cycle of poverty. It has been argued that the 'CCT model has so far failed to acknowledge the complexities of young people's trajectories' (Jones 2016, 475). Another important issue relevant to whether it will be successful is the situation on the labour market and overall economic development (Barrientos and Villa 2016). Thus, without better employment prospects, it will be difficult to reduce poverty.

Latin America, and especially Chile, were some of the first to enact pension reforms where the focus was on a private contributory pension system, but in recent years there has been a movement towards non-contributory pensions. This has happened in a variety of ways in the countries, with different levels and different conditions attached, implying that not all changes will lift people out of poverty.

Even if welfare spending can be, and is, an important aspect as a way of reducing poverty, it can also be influenced by other factors, such as transparency in government administration, absence of violence and a high electoral turnout, as has been the case, for example, in Colombia (Nieto-Aleman et al., n.d.).

Despite being a continent with a declining share of people living in poverty, it is also a continent with wide variations with many still at risk of poverty.

3.5 SUMMING-UP WHAT DO WE KNOW?

Poverty and its development vary strongly across the globe. The good news is that there has been a decline in the percentages living in absolute poverty, albeit in Africa the number is increasing due to demographic reasons. In China and India, there has been a strong reduction in the number of people living in absolute poverty.

In all the regions, there are differences among countries in what the development has been like, but the overall picture is positive. National variations can have different national causes.

In Europe, even if the number living in absolute poverty has reduced, there are still a high number of people living in relative poverty and in situations with material deprivation. Thus, there is still work to do if the aim is to eradicate poverty. This is also the case in other affluent countries such as the US and Japan.

REFERENCES

Aidukaite, Jolanta and Sven E.O. Hort. 2019. 'Editorial Introduction: Baltic States after the Crisis? The Transformation of the Welfare System and Social Problems', *Journal of Baltic Studies* 50(1): 1–6.

Alkire, Sabina and Yangyang Shen. 2017. 'Exploring Multidimensional Poverty in China: 2010 to 2014', in Sanghamitra Bandyopadhyay (ed.), *Research on Economic Inequality: Poverty, Inequality and Welfare*, 25: 161–228. Bingley: Emerald Publishing Limited.

Arza, Camila and Roxana Maurizio. 2020. 'Poverty and Social Policy in Latin America: Key Trends since c. 2000', in Bent Greve (ed.), *The Routledge International Handbook of Poverty*, 1st edn. Abingdon: Routledge.

Barrientos, Armando and Juan M. Villa. 2016. 'Economic and Political Inclusion in Human Development Conditional Income Transfer Programmes in Latin America', *Social Policy and Society* 15(3): 421–33.

Bastagli, Francesca, Jessica Hagen-Zanker, Luke Harman, Valentina Barca, Georgina Sturge and Tanja Schmidt. 2018. 'The Impact of Cash Transfers: A Review of the Evidence from Low- and Middle-Income Countries', *Journal of Social Policy*, 48(3): 569–94. https://doi.org/10.1017/S0047279418000715.

Brady, David and Amie Bostic. 2015. 'Paradoxes of Social Policy: Welfare Transfers, Relative Poverty, and Redistribution Preferences', *American Sociological Review* 80(2): 268–98. https://doi.org/10.1177/0003122415573049.

Caminada, Koen, Jinxian Wang, Kees Goudswaard, and Chen Wang. 2019. 'Relative Income Poverty Rates and Poverty Alleviation via Tax/Benefit Systems in 49 LIS Countries, 1967–2016'. Working Paper No. 761. Luxembourg: LIS Cross-National Data Center.

Causa, Orsetta and Mikkel Hermansen. 2017. 'Income Redistribution through Taxes and Transfers across OECD Countries', *OECD Economics Department Working Papers*, No. 1453. Paris: OECD Publishing.

Chuliang, Luo, Li Shi and Terry Sicular. 2018. 'The Long-Term Evolution of Income Inequality and Poverty in China', WIDER Working Paper 2018/153. Helsinki: UNU-WIDER.

Cruz-Martínez, Gibrán. 2019. *Welfare and Social Protection in Contemporary Latin America*. Abingdon: Routledge.

Datt, Gaurav, Martin Ravallion and Rinku Murgai. 2016. *Growth, Urbanization and Poverty Reduction in India*. Washington, DC: The World Bank.

Dewilde, Caroline. 2020. 'Poverty and Access to Welfare Benefits', in Bent Greve (ed.), *The Routledge International Handbook of Poverty*, 1st edn. Abingdon: Routledge.

Erk, Jan. 2017. 'Is Age the New Class? Economic Crisis and Demographics in European Politics', *Critical Sociology* 43(1): 59–71. https://doi.org/10.1177/0896920515603109.

Fontenot, Kayla, Jessica Semega and Melissa Kollar. 2018. U.S. Census Bureau, Current Population Reports, P60–263, *Income and Poverty in the United States: 2017*. Washington, DC: U.S. Government Printing Office.

Goedemé, Tim, John Hills and Bea Cantillon. 2019. *Decent Incomes for All: Improving Policies in Europe*. Oxford: Oxford University Press.

Imai, Katsushi, Raghav Gaiha and Fabrizio Bresciani. 2020. 'Dynamics of Rural Transformation and Poverty and Inequality in Asia and the Pacific', in Bent Greve (ed.), *The Routledge International Handbook of Poverty*, 1st edn. Abingdon: Routledge.

Jefferson, Philip N. 2020. 'Global Poverty: Trends, Measures, and Antidotes', in Bent Greve (ed.), *The Routledge International Handbook of Poverty*, 1st edn. Abingdon: Routledge.

Jones, Hayley. 2016. 'More Education, Better Jobs? A Critical Review of CCTs and Brazil's Bolsa Família Programme for Long-Term Poverty Reduction', *Social Policy and Society* 15(3): 465–78.

Kane, Emily. 2020. 'Poverty around the World: North America', in Bent Greve (ed.), *The Routledge International Handbook of Poverty*, 1st edn. Abingdon: Routledge.

Kane, Emily. 2018. 'The Neoliberal Baseline? A Community-Based Exploration of Beliefs about Poverty and Social Policy', *Journal of Poverty* 22(1): 65–87.

Korpi, Walter and Joakim Palme. 1998. 'The Paradox of Redistribution and Strategies of Equality: Welfare State Institutions, Inequality and Poverty in the Western Countries'. No. 174. Luxembourg: LIS Working Paper Series.

Kulkarni, Varsha S. and Raghav Gaiha. 2018. 'Beyond Piketty: A New Perspective on Poverty and Inequality in India', GDI Working Paper 2018–033. Manchester: The University of Manchester.

Matsaganis, Manos and Chrysa Leventi. 2014. 'The Distributional Impact of Austerity and the Recession in Southern Europe', *South European Society & Politics* 19(3): 393–412. http://10.0.4.56/13608746.2014.947700.

Narayan, Ambar and Rinku Murgai. 2016. *Looking Back on Two Decades of Poverty and Well-Being in India*. Washington, DC: The World Bank.

Nieto-Aleman, Paula-Andrea, Jose-Maria Garcia-Alvarez-Coque, Norat Roig-Tierno and Francisco Mas-Verdú. n.d. 'Factors of Regional Poverty Reduction in Colombia: Do Institutional Conditions Matter?' *Social Policy & Administration*. https://doi.org/10.1111/spol.12474.

Pac, Jessica, Jaehyun Nam, Jane Waldfogel and Chris Wimer. 2017. 'Young Child Poverty in the United States: Analyzing Trends in Poverty and the Role of Anti-Poverty Programs Using the Supplemental Poverty Measure', *Children and Youth Services Review* 74: 35–49.

Pantazis, Christina. 2016. 'Policies and Discourses of Poverty during a Time of Recession and Austerity.' *Critical Social Policy* 36(1): 3–20. http://10.0.4.15 3/0261018315620377.

Reich, Robert B. 2015. *Saving Capitalism: For the Many, Not the Few*. New York: Alfred E. Knopf.

Saunders, Peter. 2018. 'Monitoring and Addressing Global Poverty: A New Approach and Implications for Australia', *The Economic and Labour Relations Review* 29(1): 9–23.

Saunders, Peter and Yuvisthi Naidoo. 2018. 'Mapping the Australian Poverty Profile: A Multidimensional Deprivation Approach', *Australian Economic Review* 51(3): 336–50.

Summers, Kate. 2020. 'Poverty Development in Affluent Welfare States', in Bent Greve (ed.), *The Routledge International Handbook of Poverty*, 1st edn. Abingdon: Routledge.

Wagle, Udaya R. 2020. 'Poverty in Developing Countries, 1990–2016: Some Regional, Temporal and Income Level Variations', in Bent Greve (ed.), *The Routledge International Handbook of Poverty*, 1st edn. Abingdon: Routledge.

White, Roger and Thomas Bailleuel. 2020. 'Multidimensional Poverty Across the Life Cycle: The United States as an Empirical Example', in Bent Greve (ed.), *The Routledge International Handbook of Poverty*, 1st edn. Abingdon: Routledge.

Xue, Tao, Mark Wang and S. Rogers. 2020. 'What Contributes to a Higher Degree of Voluntarism in China's Rural Displacement Programs?', in Bent Greve (ed.), *The Routledge International Handbook of Poverty*, 1st edn. Abingdon: Routledge.

QUALITY OF LIFE FOR THOSE LIVING IN POVERTY

4.1 INTRODUCTION

The previous chapters have described the concepts and ways in which to measure and map the development in poverty. It is, however, not sufficient to understand the size of poverty, but also important to have an idea about its effect on quality of life, including how to cope with it on a daily basis. This is the focus in this chapter. It attempts to describe life for people in poverty in general, but also deals specifically with children, in-work poverty and the elderly, thus including a life and generational perspective on poverty, including the impact on the poor and their capacity for happiness. This also reflects the historical interpretation that a worker's life comprised 'five alternating periods of "want and comparative plenty, the periods of want being childhood, when he himself having had children and old age"' (Atkinson 1989, 211).

The structure of the chapter presents some cross-cutting issues related to a life in poverty (section 4.2), and sets out to examine life for children and the consequences of living in poverty both in the short- and long-term (section 4.3). The possible consequences of in-work poverty are discussed in section 4.4. The focus in section 4.5 is on the elderly, who are often seen as a specific vulnerable group. In section 4.6 there is a discussion on well-being and happiness related to income as a way of looking into quality of life at an overall level for those living in poverty. Finally, section 4.7 takes a generational perspective on the quality of life for those living in poverty, based on the presentation, and concludes up the chapter.

4.2 CROSS-CUTTING ISSUES RELATED TO A LIFE IN POVERTY

There are some general consequences of living and growing up in poverty. It is a possible cause of stigmatisation, it reduces social cohesion, and it might restrict full participation in the social and democratic life of a society. Living in poverty can also induce a feeling of shame (Gaisbauer, Schweiger and Sedmak 2019).

Those living in poverty often have worse health than those who do not. This includes hunger in the worst cases, but also poorer nutrition, lack of clean water and adequate shelter. Inequality of health is a general issue not dependent on how rich a country may be, although the consequences might be different. Those living in poverty often have more difficulties in obtaining healthcare, including sometimes not being able to pay for medication. There is a lower life expectancy for those living in poverty (Bartley 2020), and in poorer countries it is lower than in more affluent countries. It is sometimes the case that life expectancy varies strongly within a city and country (Bambra 2016).

Those living in poverty will, less often than others, gain an education, even in countries where access to education is free of charge. This can then have long-term consequences for access to the development of human and social capital, and thereby decreased access to the labour market.

It is often the case that people with low incomes participate less in society and they have a slightly higher risk of crime, and fewer social relations. This is because an increase in inequality and social polarisation reduces social networks, and this has the strongest impact on the poor (Christoforou and Davis 2014). Increased segregation and marginalisation can have the same impact (Putnam 2016).

Higher income and reduced poverty might also reduce stress-related abuse, including violence against women (Bastagli et al. 2018). So, life conditions are generally improved where poverty is reduced.

4.3 IMPACT ON CHILDREN LIVING IN POVERTY

The United Nations Convention on the Rights of the Child came into force in 1990, with the aim of protecting the basic human rights of children, including additional protocols to ensure better lives for all young persons.[1] However, it is still the case that many children grow up in poverty, as shown in Chapter 2. This is also shown in several studies from UNICEF showing that there are the following numbers of children living in absolute poverty (using the $1.9 per day level) for the different age groups:

0–4 years – 122 million
5–9 years – 118 million
10–14 years – 99 million
15–17 years – 46 million[2]

Thus, it is a very large number of children. There are also many living in relative poverty in the richer parts of the world, and in the aftermath of the financial crisis there was an increase in these numbers (Cantillon et al. 2017). A life in poverty can be very difficult, and even more so for children, as they are unable to live the same fulfilling life as other children (Gray 2020; Lancker and Vinck 2020).

A child in such a household might have fewer options to participate in activities, including sport or other extracurricular types of activities. This lack of participation poses the risk of a lower level attainment of education and thereby fewer opportunities later in life, in line with the understanding of the capability approach (Sen 2005).

A child growing up in a poor household will experience lower levels of nutrition, and perhaps periods of hunger, thus also risking poorer health than those children growing up in more affluent families. The impact can be seen throughout the life course by, among other things, a lower than average life expectancy in poorer countries than in rich countries. Also, teenagers living in poverty may endure persistent lower incomes in later life (Lesner 2018).

The many and varied consequences for children of growing up in poverty are the reason why one needs to be aware of how to deal with it, given that the consequences are also long-lasting. This has therefore been argued to be a good case for social investment due to the high returns in trying to prevent these negative consequences (Heckman 2006). Even though there has been criticism of this (Rea and Burton 2018), it is an indication that growing up as a child in poverty might have negative long-term possibilities and thus a negative impact both for individuals and for society. There is apparently an association with growing up in a jobless household (often, therefore, also living in poverty) and long-term impact on educational attainment, later unemployment and living in poverty, which is the case in most countries in Europe (Macmillan et al. 2018).

In the US, close to one in five children live in poverty, which is double that of developed countries. It has been argued that part of the reason is an increase in the divorce rate (Komlos 2018), and that altered family structures and prevalence of single parent households might be contributory factors for children to be living in poverty.

In several developed countries, single parents have the right to child maintenance support from the child's other parent in order to reduce the risk of living in poverty. However, it seems that in a number of countries (data from 2013) the interaction with the social welfare system means that this is not the case, and, further, that in some countries the 'states retain all, or a proportion of child maintenance in order to offset other fiscal costs' (Hakovirta et al., n.d., 2).

Children growing up in poverty have lower levels of well-being, see on this topic also section 4.6. There is often a lower level of education, a lower labour market attachment later in life, the risk of health problems and an increased likelihood of being in need of benefit in adult life. Children growing up in poverty might, to a larger degree than others, also be living in dependency when they have grown up.

4.4 IN-WORK POVERTY A PROBLEM?

In general, it is assumed, at least in the most affluent countries, that being employed will ensure that a person is able to live a life without poverty. This is on the assumption that the wage level is sufficiently high for disposable income to be above the poverty line. Recent years have seen a widening difference in wages on the labour market (Cohen and Ladaique 2018), the result of which is that having a job does not necessarily mean an income above the poverty level and having a job is not always protection against poverty (Marx 2020).

There can be a number of reasons for this. The first is that the wage level, even if there are legal rules on the minimum wage (see further on regulations, Chapter 5), can be so low that income will not be sufficiently high to avoid living in poverty and it might not be possible to achieve the minimum income if work is undertaken in the informal sector of the labour market. The ability to avoid being part of the 'working poor' will also depend on how many persons the income needs to support. Thus, using the equivalised disposable income (see Chapter 2) might mean that even a full-time working person still cannot support the family. This is especially the case for single parents and, especially in several countries, single women. A change in family formation and risk of divorce are challenges which mean that for some, this will cause a life in poverty, including for the children. The consequences for children (see more in section 4.3), are undoubtedly negative.

Given the knowledge on how unequal societies negatively influence societal development on a number of parameters (Wilkinson and Pickett 2009; Stiglitz 2012), there is no doubt that this will also be the case with regard to those working poor. It might even be more stigmatising and stressful to have a full-time job, a low income and a family to provide for and then not be able to ensure an income above the poverty line. There is further the risk that the combined impact of changes in taxes and social security benefits, even if working, might still make it difficult to avoid living in poverty, i.e. what is labelled 'the poverty trap'. This further also reflects the fact that there is a risk of low-take up, i.e. people do not get the benefit they could, in principle, be eligible for as they do not know about it, or do not apply for it due to a lack of, among other things, social capital.

Working poor can also be applied to those who are either voluntarily part-time, may be forced to work part-time and thereby either not willing or able to obtain full-time work. Thus, working part-time can cause a higher risk of being working poor. This can be difficult, particularly for lone parents and single people. This reflects a challenge for the impact of the way the labour market functions, and there is a risk that this will increase in the future with the development of the platform economy (Hill 2015; Greve 2017). The increased pressure from technology might mean that more people will be at risk of working poor, albeit so far this is only to a more limited extent. However, we have seen that the increase in inequality and poverty has been strongly influenced by the development on the labour market (Caminada et al. 2019).

If access to health care is highly dependent on being on the labour market, as it is in the US, then this can mean that some accept very low paying jobs if this improves their access to health care, and thereby reduces possible concern about not having a sufficiently good health care cover. In the US, it is also the case that there has been a growth in the working poor, and the earned income tax credit has been expanded, but given one needs to have a job to get it, then this helps only to a limited extent in alleviating poverty, which is also indicated by the fact that in 2012, 31 per cent of those receiving food stamps were in work (Reich 2015).

Not only those employed can be at risk of working poor, but also those doing what has been termed 'bogus self-employment' are at risk. This is also due to the fact that self-employed people might not have any support from national minimum income legislation or a collective agreement. Self-employment can thereby be a new group at risk, which formally was looked upon as working, but in reality, having such a low income that they are more or less permanently in a situation of living in poverty.

Besides the risk of being working poor in the official economy, this can also be due to informal employment, which is understood as jobs where there is no compliance with existing rules, including in relation to wage, social welfare protection, etc. It is estimated that around the globe more than two billion people work in these conditions,[3] mainly in emerging and developing countries. Thus, in-work poverty is not only related to having a job in the formal economy, but also within the informal economy. This also includes own-account workers. Informal employment is the highest in Africa and in general in the developing and emerging countries as argued above. In these countries it is close to 100 per cent for those not having any education. It is also high for those having non-standard jobs, and it is often higher for those only having a limited number of working hours, as part-time workers have a higher risk.[4]

The risk of working poor is typically higher in countries with weaker labour movements. Table 4.1 shows the risk of working poor for those having a high work-intensity (defined as between 0.85 and

Table 4.1 At risk of in-work poverty within EU countries in selected years since 2010

GEO/TIME	2010	2013	2015	2017
European Union - 28 countries	4,5	4,8	5,2	5,2
Belgium	2,4	1,9	2,9	2,6
Bulgaria	3,1	2,3	2,8	4,2
Czechia	2,1	2,4	2,8	2,4
Denmark	5,1	4,1	4,0	3,5
Germany	4,4	5,2	5,5	4,9
Estonia	4,3	4,8	7,1	7,9
Ireland	2,8	1,7	1,5	2,5
Greece	7,3	4,0	5,2	4,3
Spain	4,9	5,0	6,3	6,8
France	3,5	4,1	4,5	4,1
Croatia	2,0	2,3	1,2	1,8
Italy	3,6	5,4	4,9	7,0
Cyprus	5,4	5,8	4,3	3,8
Latvia	5,7	5,3	5,8	4,9
Lithuania	8,2	5,5	6,1	4,8
Luxembourg	7,0	7,2	8,0	9,5
Hungary	2,0	2,3	5,9	8,0
Malta	1,6	0,8	1,7	1,5
Netherlands	2,9	2,5	1,0	2,7
Austria	4,8	4,8	4,8	4,8
Poland	6,9	6,0	6,5	6,3
Portugal	4,0	5,5	5,6	5,7
Romania	12,9	12,2	12,5	11,1
Slovenia	3,2	3,6	3,5	4,0
Slovakia	4,3	3,2	3,8	4,7
Finland	2,1	2,4	2,3	1,6
Sweden	5,2	5,0	6,3	4,8
United Kingdom	3,2	3,7	4,2	3,7

1, e.g. least working 85 per cent of what is considered full-time work) for the EU countries.

The level and development are very uneven across Europe. In 2017, it varied between 1.5 per cent in Malta to 11.1 per cent in Romania.

From a development with a decline of 3.4 percentage points in Lithuania to an increase of six per cent in Hungary. There is further no clear pattern across welfare regimes and countries hit by the financial crisis, and even after recovery in several countries since 2015 there has been continued increase in those at risk of in-work poverty. A country hard hit such as Greece has seen a decline in the risk, whereas there has been an increase in Spain, Italy and Portugal. Still, the table shows the risk of working poor even applies to those having a high work-intensity. For those working part-time it is up to one-third of all having the risk. So, as indicated above, one reason is work-intensity, but it is not the full story, and the possible increase in precariousness on the labour market might make working poor a new and important issue in many countries.

The risk of working poor is thus very unevenly distributed among people living in different types of welfare states. This is not only due to the situation on the labour market, but also the possibility of different kinds of benefits that might top up what has been earned as wage income, see more in Chapter 5 on benefits in-cash and in-kind.

4.5 POVERTY IN OLD AGE

Historically, the elderly were often provided for by living together with the family, and their life expectancy was also considerably lower than it is today. Reduction of old age poverty was a central aim of welfare states after the Second World War. Today, reaching old age and no longer being part of the labour market can result in living with limited financial means, although some have been able to save money to spend in old age. However, in many welfare states, the position has improved and there has been a decline in the poverty rate (Ebbinghaus, Nelson and Nieuwenhuis 2020), albeit with exceptions in countries such as Australia, Switzerland and the UK. The degree of change further varies from country to country.

In the OECD area, those having the highest risk of poverty are, as in many other welfare states, single persons, migrants and those with a low level of education. Thus, there is an intersection with the other risks of living in poverty.

In most welfare states, the main support for the elderly is pensions, but can in principle also be support for accommodation, cheap transport and health care (free or with high levels of subsidy). However, those who have a very low income might be less able to get the necessary food and might also have stronger difficulties in being part of the overall societal development.

Pension systems and their ability to support the elderly vary across welfare regimes, albeit support to the elderly in general is one of the welfare areas with a high degree of legitimacy (Greve 2019). This is not the place to delve into the detail of pension systems (Hinrichs 2019), but age of retirement, replacement rate of pension and other types of support to the elderly also influence the risk. Overall, the pension system is an important issue with regard to the ability to reduce the risk of living in poverty (Been et al. 2016;Vliet et al. 2020; Jacques, Leroux, and Stevanovic 2018). Since the 1990s in a number of more mature welfare states, there has been a reduction in the generosity of pensions, including a change that pensions should depend on contributions (Grech 2015).

One point to be aware of, however, is that if the pension system is related to having a long career in full employment, then this will be a disadvantage for those having a more interrupted working life. If the size of the pension further depends on income during the working life, this will also be a disadvantage for low-income earners. Further, if the system does not take into consideration time taken out of employment to care for children, then this could be a disadvantage for women.

There can also be differences between public and private pension systems, thus analysis points out that the use of private pensions will cause a higher poverty level than the use of a public pension system, based upon data in OECD countries from 1995 to 2011 (Been et al. 2016).The analysis also points out that more public sector and higher levels of spending in welfare states can be an indicator of how many are living in poverty.

Thereby, it is not sufficient to focus on the fact that there may be a pension system in a country; the parameters for achieving the pension and the size thereof can also be important in order to gauge the risk of living in poverty for people in old age.

4.6 HAPPINESS AND POVERTY

Overall, the situation is that on average, people living in richer countries are happier than those living in poorer countries.[5] In general, it is also the case that when income grows, happiness does too, although only to a certain level, otherwise known as the Easterlin paradox (Easterlin 2013; Greve 2011). This includes not only absolute poverty, but also the relative position in a society (Ejrnæs and Greve 2017), as well as the fact that financial crises can have a negative impact on well-being (Greve 2012).

Therefore, one would in general have the expectation that happier people live in richer countries, and thereby that those living in poverty will be even less happy in very poor countries. This need not always be the case, as a study from India showed that the young living in the poorer area of Calcutta were happier than those in the more affluent areas (Martin 2002). Although, overall, there is a clear connection so that if, for example, it would be possible to reduce the number of people living in absolute poverty one should, all other things being equal, be able to find that people around the globe are happier than before.

Thus, a life lived in poverty not only has material consequences, but also influences the quality of life. This is not only happiness, but also vital access to water and sanitation, which for example, is included in the UNDP multidimensional poverty index, see http://hdr.undp.org/en/2018-MPI. Water quality is, as another example, also included in the OECD's better life index, see www.oecdbetterlifeindex.org/topics/environment/, as indicating that quality of life is influenced by aspects other than money. However, being an affluent country increases the likelihood that elements other than money influence life for those in poverty. Thus, the relatively rich Nordic welfare states are typically at the top of the list of the happiest countries around the globe. Table 4.2 shows the five happiest countries and the five least happy in 2019.

Thus, there is no doubt that countries with high levels of poverty are also countries with a lower level of happiness, even though also issues such as civil war and good governance can have an impact on quality of life.

Table 4.2 The five most and least happy nations in 2019

Finland	7,8
Denmark	7,6
Norway	7,6
Iceland	7,5
Netherlands	7,5
Rwanda	3,3
Tanzania	3,2
Afghanistan	3,2
Central African Republic	3,1
South Sudan	2,8

Source: Available at http://worldhappiness.report/ed/2019/, accessed 9 April 2019.

Note: Respondents were asked to think of a ladder, with best possible life for themselves being 10, and the worst possible being 0. They were asked to rate their lives on a scale of 0–10. The data represents average of all interviews conducted 2016–2018.

In studies of happiness, it can be difficult to be sure about the causality; however, there seems to be no doubt about the fact that a life in poverty also influences the quality of life, so that a reduction will improve happiness.

4.7 SUMMING-UP – A GENERATIONAL PERSPECTIVE

It is difficult to cope with a life lived in poverty, and life expectancy of those in poverty is often reduced as a result. Growing up in poverty can cause reduced opportunities later on in life, including the ability to achieve a proper education and stable employment. So, even if there are stages over the life-cycle where the risk of living in poverty is higher than in other stages, this is one of the times where it might have a longer lasting impact than at later stages.

This does not imply that it is easy to be working poor, which in fact might also have an effect on children. Neither is it easy to reach old age and have no income, and thereby those who are frail might have difficulties in getting the necessary support in order to have a decent life.

There are not only day-to-day issues for people living at risk of poverty, but there are also long-term implications, and a risk that periods of time spent in poverty can also influence other parts of one's life. This is witnessed by the lower level of happiness in poorer countries.

NOTES

1 See www.ohchr.org/en/professionalinterest/pages/crc.aspx, for more information.
2 See www.unicef.org/publications/index_92826.html, accessed 4 April 2019.
3 See www.ilo.org/global/about-the-ilo/newsroom/news/WCMS_627189/lang—en/index.htm, accessed 27 March 2019.
4 www.ilo.org/global/publications/books/WCMS_626831/lang—en/index.htm, accessed 28 March 2019.
5 See for the position of the world's countries: World Happiness Report, published annually at http://worldhappiness.report/download/.

REFERENCES

Atkinson, Tony. 1989. 'Poverty', in John Eatwell, Murray Milgate and Peter Newman (eds), *The New Palgrave Social Economics*, 2nd edn. Basingstoke: Palgrave Macmillan, pp. 204–14.

Bambra, Clare. 2016. *Health Divides – Where You Live Can Kill You*. Bristol: Policy Press.

Bartley, Mel. 2020. 'Poverty and Health Inequality', in Bent Greve (ed.), *The Routledge International Handbook of Poverty*, 1st edn. Abingdon: Routledge.

Bastagli, Francesca, Jessica Hagen-Zanker, Luke Harman, Valentina Barca, Georgina Sturge and Tanja Schmidt. 2018. 'The Impact of Cash Transfers: A Review of the Evidence from Low- and Middle-Income Countries', *Journal of Social Policy*, 48(3): 569–94. https://doi.org/10.1017/S0047279418000715.

Been, Jim, Koen Caminada, Kees Goudswaard, and Olaf van Vliet. 2016. 'Public/Private Pension Mix, Income Inequality and Poverty among the Elderly in Europe: An Empirical Analysis Using New and Revised OECD Data', *Social Policy & Administration* 51(7): 1079–1100. https://doi.org/10.1111/spol.12282.

Caminada, Koen, Jinxian Wang, Kees Goudswaard, and Chen Wang. 2019. 'Relative Income Poverty Rates and Poverty Alleviation via Tax/Benefit Systems in 49 LIS-Countries, 1967–2016', Working Paper No. 761. Luxembourg: LIS Cross-National Data Center.

Cantillon, Bea, Yekateria Chzhen, Sudhanshu Handa and Brian Nolan. 2017. *Children of Austerity: Impact of the Great Recession on Child Poverty in Rich Countries*. Oxford: Oxford University Press.

Christoforou, Asimina and John B. Davis. 2014. 'Social Capital: Social Values, Power, and Social Identity', in Asimina Christoforou and John B. Davis (eds) *Social Capital and Economics, Social Values, Power, and Social Identity*. Abingdon: Routledge, pp. 25–34.

Cohen, Guillaume and Maxime Ladaique. 2018. 'Drivers of Growing Income Inequalities in OECD and European Countries', in Renato Miguel Carmo, Cédric Rio and Márton Medgyesi (eds), *Reducing Inequalities: A Challenge for the European Union?* Cham: Springer International Publishing, pp. 1–43. https://doi.org/10.1007/978-3-319-65006-7_3.

Easterlin, Richard A. 2013. 'Happiness, Growth and Public Policy', IZA Discussion Paper No. 7234. Bonn: IZA.

Ebbinghaus, Bernhard, Kenneth Nelson and Rense Nieuwenhuis. 2020. 'Poverty in Old Age', in Bent Greve (ed.), *The Routledge International Handbook of Poverty*, 1st edn. Abingdon: Routledge.

Ejrnæs, Anders and Bent Greve. 2017. 'Your Position in Society Matters for How Happy You Are', *International Journal of Social Welfare* 26(3): 206–17. https://doi.org/10.1111/ijsw.12233.

Gaisbauer, Helmut, Gottfried Schweiger and Clemens Sedmak. 2019. *Absolute Poverty in Europe*. Bristol: Policy Press.

Gray, Jane, Jennifer Dagg and Clíona Rooney. 2020. 'Coping with Poverty – Life for People', in Bent Greve (ed.), *The Routledge International Handbook of Poverty*, 1st edn. Abingdon: Routledge.

Grech, Aaron. 2015. 'Evaluating the Possible Impact of Pension Reforms on Elderly Poverty in Europe', *Social Policy & Administration* 49(1): 68–87.

Greve, Bent. 2011. *Happiness*. Abingdon: Routledge.

Greve, Bent. 2012. 'The Impact of the Financial Crisis on Happiness in Affluent European Countries', *Journal of Comparative Social Welfare* 28(3): 183–93. https://doi.org/10.1080/17486831.2012.736354.

Greve, Bent. 2017. *Technology and the Future of Work. The Impact on Labour Markets and Welfare States.* Cheltenham: Edward Elgar.

Greve, Bent. 2019. *Welfare Populism and Welfare Chauvinism*. Bristol: Policy Press.

Hakovirta, Mia, Christine Skinner, Heikki Hiilamo and Merita Jokela. 2019. 'Child Poverty, Child Maintenance and Interactions with Social Assistance Benefits Among Lone Parent Families: A Comparative Analysis.' *Journal of Social Policy*, March: 1–21. https://doi.org/10.1017/S0047279419000151.

Heckman, James J. 2006. 'Skill Formation and the Economics of Investing in Disadvantaged Children', *Science* 312: 1900–1902.

Hill, Steven. 2015. *Raw Deal. How the "Uber Economy" and Runaway Capitalism Are Screwing American Workers*. New York: St. Martin's Press.

Hinrichs, Karl. 2019. 'Old Age and Pensions', in Bent Greve (ed.) *The Routledge Handbook of the Welfare State*, 2nd edn, Abingdon: Routledge, pp. 418–31.

Jacques, Philippe, Marie-Louise Leroux and Dalibor Stevanovic. 2018. 'Poverty Among the Elderly: The Role of Public Pension Systems', Working paper, No. 18–07. Québec: Cahiers de Recherche.

Komlos, John. 2018. *Foundations of Real World Economics: What Every Economics Student Needs to Know*. Abingdon: Routledge.

Lancker, Wim van and Julie Vinck. 2020. 'The Consequence of Growing up Poor', in Bent Greve (ed.), *The Routledge International Handbook of Poverty*, 1st edn. Abingdon: Routledge.

Lesner, Rune V. 2018. 'The Long-Term Effect of Childhood, *Journal of Population Economics* 31(3): 969–1004. https://doi.org/10.1007/s00148-017-0674-8.

Macmillan, Lindsay, Paul Gregg, John Jerrim and Nikki Shure. 2018. 'Children in Jobless Households across Europe: Evidence on the Association with Medium- and Long-Term Outcomes', *Journal of Poverty and Social Justice* 26(3): 335–58.

Martin, Seligman. 2002. *Authentic Happiness: Using the New Positive Psychology to Realize Your Potential for Lasting Fulfillment*. New York: Free Press.

Marx, Ive. 2020. 'Working Poor', in Bent Greve (ed.), *The Routledge International Handbook of Poverty*, 1st edn. Abingdon: Routledge.

Putnam, Robert D. 2016. *Our Kids: The American Dream in Crisis*. New York: Simon and Schuster.

Rea, David and Tony Burton. 2018. 'Does an Empirical Heckman Curve Exist?', Working Papers, Institute for Governance Reform, Victoria University, Wellington, NZ.

Reich, Robert B. 2015. *Saving Capitalism: For the Many, Not the Few*. New York: Alfred E. Knopf.

Sen, Amartya. 2005. 'Human Rights and Capabilities', *Journal of Human Development* 6(2): 151–66. https://doi.org/10.1080/14649880500120491.

Stiglitz, Joseph E. 2012. *The Price of Inequality: How Today's Divided Society Endangers Our Future*. New York: W.W. Norton & Company.

Vliet, Olaf van, Koen Caminada, Kees Goudswaard, and Jixian Wang. 2020. 'Poverty Reduction among Older People through Pensions: A Comparative Analysis', in Bent Greve (ed.), *The Routledge International Handbook of Poverty*, 1st edn. Abingdon: Routledge.

Wilkinson, Richard G. and Pickett, Kate. 2009. *The Spirit Level – Why Equality Is Better for Everyone*. London: Allen Lane.

EXPLANATION OF AND POSSIBLE POLICIES AIMED AT REDUCING POVERTY

5.1 INTRODUCTION

There is, presumably, not one single policy that might help in eradicating poverty. Section 5.2 presents a few typical explanations of poverty as a starting point for discussing policies aimed at poverty such as changes at the labour market, including the risk of working poor, as presented in Chapter 4. Migration as a consequence of poverty in individual countries is discussed later in Chapter 6, as well as international organisations and policies.

There are a variety of possible instruments available if there is the will to reduce poverty. This begins with the discussion in section 5.3 as to whether it is possible to prevent poverty from arising. Section 5.4 shows several of the instruments that might, in principle, be used to reduce poverty, including a variety of social safety nets, education, welfare services and the impact of the choice of taxes and duties. Existing evidence of how a set of instruments might reduce poverty is provided. The section also looks into how some policies have actually been used, including elements such as the level of welfare benefits and services, pensions, education, health services and support to families with children, but also other possible conditions related to receiving those benefits. Section 5.5 then discusses the by now classical issue of whether a targeted approach will have a better impact on equality and poverty than a broader approach (Korpi and Palme 1998).

5.2 WHY DO WE HAVE POVERTY?

There can be a number of reasons for the fact that we still have poverty. A historical distinction and discussion, still in evidence today, considers structural and behavioural reasons (Bradshaw 2000). This can also be systematised into:

1 Individual factors: lack of effort, lack of motivation, money mismanagement.
2 Structural factors: poor education, insufficient opportunities, an economic system that favours the rich.
3 Uncontrollable factors: fate, bad luck.

(Leiser and Shemesh 2018, 89)

This shows that there can be, and presumably are, many and varied explanations. They can and will, presumably, also change over time. So, it is not necessarily a stable situation, and further it can vary between countries, and even within countries it might be that all the factors influence part of the development in poverty.

Looking into structural reasons, these relate to the fact that one can look at change in societal structures that cause, for example, loss of jobs and as a result a slide into subsequent poverty, at least if there are no existing social service safety nets.

Change on the labour market in the wake of structural causes might thus be a reason for the number of people living in poverty, as some people for a number of possible reasons (educational attainment level, geography and age) are not able to get a new job. This can also be presented as a difference between supply and demand sides approaches with regard to labour market development. The supply side would focus on the willingness to work (i.e. to supply one's labour), whereas the demand side is linked to whether there is, in fact, a demand for workers. For both demand and supply side there is the question whether even if having a job, if on a low wage is enough to avoid living in poverty, i.e. the working poor issue.

Naturally, development towards a state of poverty and the number of people living in poverty can be due to the lack of a sufficiently developed support system to those in need of finding work or otherwise avoid living in poverty.

Another explanation has focused on the fact that people may not be willing to work, i.e. a self-responsibility argument. This has its roots in classical discussions on who is deserving and who is not (Will 1993; van Oorschot 2006), but also on the perspective of the underclass (Murray and Field 1990). This has been discussed for a long time, it has even been argued that Elizabeth I was the first to make this distinction (Romano 2017), who also quotes St Paul: 'we gave you this rule: the one who is unwilling to work shall not eat' (p. 16).

The labour market and civil society also play a role. The market, due to the fact that increased inequality in the market and low levels of income and working poor might be factors, for which see Chapter 4. Civil society plays a role in the sense that family and/or philanthropy might support those in need. The transfer of economic resources within civil society might thus alleviate part of the risk of living in poverty, and, in fact this is the case even without the possibility of having solid data in this respect. Philanthropic support to reduce poverty is possible, but again we have limited data; who receives this support is under private consideration and not subject to the influence of societal preferences.

Change in family structure can also influence poverty, given that a single parent household to a larger degree is at risk of living in poverty, and whether people are at risk of living in poverty is also influenced by the economic transfers within a family (Daly 2018). Thus, for example, using equivalence scales (see Chapter 2) presumes that there is equal sharing within a family, and this need not to be the case. This also helps in explaining that persons not included in the income statistics for those living in poverty might still be living in poverty if the intra-household distribution is not taking place (Daly 2018).

Naturally, there are also a number of obstacles to remove poverty at the global level. These include:

a) Inequality and limited redistribution.
b) Ineffective education.

c) Restricted access to Healthcare.
d) Violence and Conflict: Civil and International Wars.

(Jefferson 2020).

These elements, especially a) and b) are a central part of the issues used in relation to the discussion below of policies that might help to combat poverty. Healthcare is touched upon in several places in this book, and it is also obvious that violence and conflict are important, but this is a matter for mainly international political discussions, whereas the instruments presented below are things that can be achieved if money and the will are in place.

5.3 PREVENTING POVERTY

'An ounce of prevention is worth a pound of cure' (Benjamin Franklin, 1735) is much quoted but the general failure to put more effort into prevention continues. 'Everyone says that prevention is better than cure, and hardly anyone acts as if he believes it'.

(Mackintosh, on ill-health, 1953, 5),
here from (Sinfield 2020, 1)

Thus, despite the fact that prevention in social policy has been considered a central aspect for a long time (Berghman, Debels and Van Hoyweghen 2019), this is perhaps still not central in the ways in which to cope with and deal with poverty, and in the context that the aim is that spending now will be more economical than spending later. With regard to government policies of prevention, these take time to implement; it might make it more difficult to get sufficient support for such policies as they could potentially damage certainty of re-election. Furthermore, if the reason for poverty by some is seen as some not wanting or being able to get out of poverty, there might not be sufficient will and effort to do something about it. It might not be a populist policy to reduce poverty (Greve 2019), unless it can be seen as part of a wider issue of supporting groups seen as being deserving of support from the welfare state.

There is also the issue about being sure of what and how are the most effective ways of being able to prevent poverty from increasing, given that this might be due to, for example, technological change. It will presumably also be difficult to prevent poverty arising in cases of national emergency and war.

Another issue is how to be sure to have the necessary instruments in place to prevent people ending up living in poverty. However, given what we know it seems obvious that an early intervention for children would be cost-effective (Heckman 2006), even though this has been questioned by recent studies, as also argued in Chapter 4. Still, knowledge about what works and what does not work is also important with regard to these interventions, given the drive to get most value for the available resources. The reason why prevention might be difficult to measure with regard to poverty is that the precise counterfactual situation is often not available, and further that the necessary data are also lacking (Greve 2017a).

It further seems logical that investment in social and human capital, including high levels of education, can be strong policies if the aim is for long-term prevention and avoidance of poverty. Therefore, ensuring sufficient resources for education can be an important aspect.

Wealthier countries have, as we have seen earlier, a lower level of absolute poverty, and thus the ability to increase economic growth might be one way to gain more resources also for those living below the absolute poverty line. Thus, also questioning whether one can legitimately argue for non-economic growth, as this would especially be a problem for those in need of more economic resources. This is aptly described in a book about inequality, see *Ferraris for All. In Defence of Economic Progress* (Ben-Ami 2012).

However, even if economic growth is achieved and reduces absolute poverty, then whether this will have an impact on the level of relative poverty is influenced by how that gain from growth is distributed. If increased wealth is going to those already above the line, then the impact on poverty will naturally be less effective or even non-existent.

Therefore, economic growth is not a sufficient condition for a reduction of poverty (Alkire et al. 2015); there is also a need for political will to use a variety of instruments, which is the focus of the next section, that might reduce the level of poverty. This also includes, in principle, a labour market policy of having a job, even though the risk of working poor can be an important element in preventing poverty. This despite the fact that from 2001 to 2007 most

European countries were seemingly better at increasing employment than reducing poverty (Taylor-Gooby, Gumy and Otto 2015), pointing to the fact that prevention is not only achieved by creating more jobs, but also by creating better, more well-paid jobs.

5.4 INSTRUMENTS TO COPE WITH POVERTY

Naturally, strategies created to reduce poverty can function at very different levels, ranging from macro-economic policies (increasing job creation, competitiveness, etc); the meso-level, restructuring of the public sector to divert spending away from those areas not necessarily assisting in the alleviation of poverty; to the micro-level, including education, micro-credit, etc. (Addison, Hulme, and Kanbur 2009). Here the focus is mainly on public sector direct interventions through different kinds of benefits and services. However, also a few other elements, such as different regulations, are presented as well. This section is split into different sections in order to present a number of possible instruments that can be used if the aim is to reduce the level of poverty, including discussions on not only intended, but also possible unintended effects of the policy. However, in order not to lose sight of the main focus, the distinction is between benefits in-kind and in-cash and the financing of the policies to combat poverty. There is a specific section on education, given the possible impact this might have on the longer-term impact on poverty, also as argued above it might be an instrument to prevent poverty, but it might further increase the likelihood of reducing it if it arises.

There is a discussion on the impact of social protection and economic growth. An argument has been that high levels of social protection, and thereby support to those living in poverty, could reduce economic growth. However, this seems not to be the case as, among other things, benefits to the poor increase demand for goods and services, and also make it more likely that they will be actively involved in society (Deeming and Smyth 2018). Several studies from international organisations also confirm that reducing inequality should not have a negative impact on economic development, and might even have a positive impact (Cournède, Fournier, and Hoeller 2018; OECD 2015).

Good governance and a stable institutional structure can also be important, given that this can help in having a more efficient administration, better use of resources and perhaps also help in a more peaceful development.

5.4.1 CASH BENEFITS AND POVERTY

Overall, it seems that the size of the budget available for social purposes reduces the level of inequality (Caminada et al. 2019; Brady and Bostic 2015; Walter Korpi and Palme 2003). Thereby, available resources for cash benefit distributed to those below the set poverty line is, in principle, a possible way to reduce poverty, which then implies that the willingness to collect taxes and duties has an implication on the impact on, and the size of, poverty.

However, the size of the budget might be important, but the impact may also be influenced by different types of conditions attached to the right to receive cash benefit, including the criteria for eligibility. This can include searching for work, participating in education (in principle, also for children in the family), having no wealth, etc., see also in section 3.4.3 on the CCT programme in South America. Naturally, the size of the benefit also influences how many it is possible to lift out of poverty, either as a consequence of low income on the labour market or when being outside the labour market (unemployed, retired, under-educated, etc.).

As the size of the benefit might, theoretically, influence behaviour (especially work and saving) then this will often be a balance between efficiency and equity also compared to those working, so that there remains an incentive to take up employment. The literature does not in itself inform about how large the difference should be, but it opens the way for the fact that there might be a need for at least some difference. This is, in fact, also the case in all welfare states, given that the replacement rate is below 100.

Both the size of the cash benefit and conditions attached to receiving it might vary depending on the age group receiving it, cf. also in Chapter 3, that poverty can vary across the life cycle, and some persons are seen as more deserving than others. There might thus, to take just one example, be less stringent demands attached to receiving old-age pension than to unemployment benefit and social assistance.

The conditionality often also depends on the type of system, as in an insurance-based system, which might have fewer conditions when the actual situation occurs than in a different system. In other types, there might be more conditionality attached including means-testing of the benefit – which can be against income in the household and/ or wealth.

Child benefit or different types of family allowances, where the intention is to support the quality of life for children, can have other criteria attached than what is typical for other types of cash benefit. Child benefits are not only a redistribution towards children and with the purpose of reducing poverty but are, in principle, also a reallocation of resources from families without children to families with children. Again, the size of the benefits, whether they are means-tested or not, is open for political decisions and preferences on where to spend the available budget on social policy.

For elderly people, the pension system is an important factor in reducing poverty levels among older aged people. A recent study showed that in countries covered by LIS data, 56 per cent were lifted out of poverty in 2013 through the tax benefit system (the main component being the pension) (Vliet et al. 2020, see also Been et al. 2016; Jacques, Leroux and Stevanovic 2018).

It is not only in developed welfare states in richer countries that cash transfers are used as part of poverty alleviation strategies. In a study covering low- and middle-income countries using selected criteria for monetary poverty (such as household expenditure, food expenditure, poverty headcount, poverty gap), it was shown that transfers reduce poverty and increase the likelihood of an increase in food expenditure (and total expenditure). Thus, transfers seemingly have a more general impact on poverty across countries using cash transfers (Bastagli et al. 2018). In the EU, the reduction of poverty for lone parents, i.e. also thereby in poverty for children, it seems that the more generous welfare states have lower child poverty (Chzhen and Bradshaw 2012), and in general that welfare generosity implies lower levels of poverty (Saltkjel and Malmberg-Heimonen 2017), although data are from 2009.

An analysis of seven different EU countries has shown that the most cost-effective way to reduce poverty is to increase child benefits and social assistance, and, at the same time, that reducing child benefits through budget cuts will increase poverty. This is not necessarily of the same size in all countries, but the direction is the same (Leventi, Sutherland and Valentinova Tasseva 2017). It is further the case that income transfers might not only reduce the number of people living in poverty, but can also reduce relative deprivation (Goedemé, Hills and Cantillon 2019).

Overall, one can still argue that it is possible, in principle, to use benefits to lift people with disposable income below the set line (both absolute and relative) above the poverty line if there are economic resources available, legitimacy and the political will to do so. It is also the case that this, in a sense, can be argued to mean a more individualised poverty perspective. In the Global South, cash transfers are still limited and might even have a negative impact in certain circumstances, and in many countries they are somewhat fragmented and exclude certain groups (Leisering 2020).

5.4.2 IN-KIND BENEFITS – SERVICES AND POVERTY

Even if, as argued above, a variation in cash-benefits can lift people out of poverty, then this is less certain when looking into a number of welfare services, i.e. in-kind benefits. One problem is that it is difficult to monetise the value of the services, and thereby to include the level in the measurement of whose disposable income is below the set level. Still, it might have an impact on the risk for those whose income is below the poverty line, and by this too on the overall quality of life.

For example, access to childcare at an affordable price might increase the likelihood of being able to hold down a job on the labour market. Thus, a single parent's ability to ensure an income above the poverty line can be increased by the availability of such a welfare service. Given that single parents, usually women, in most countries need to work in order to have a chance to get an income above the poverty line, if childcare is not available or very expensive this would be difficult. Welfare services might be a useful option for supporting people in such a way that they do not, perhaps, need income transfers.

Other types of in-kind benefit which could exert a positive impact could include inexpensive transport, housing or other essential daily amenities, including water, electricity and heating. Free healthcare can also be an important boost for low-income households as they might otherwise not be able to get the necessary help when they are in need. Food banks have also been a way of supporting poor people, although the impact and consequences are less clear (Purdam, Garratt and Esmail 2016; Middleton et al. 2018; Lambie-Mumford 2019). The development being a consequence of that lack of food security can be a strong issue for people in poverty and in-kind support (which can be both public and private) through food banks might, for some, even given the risk of stigma attached, be an option to obtain food. It is, if used instead of income transfers, a paternalistic way of supporting people in poverty, as they do not have a choice of what they prefer, as others do. This is an example also of a policy where there is no solid evidence that it is an effective way of solving the issue of food insecurity (Middleton et al. 2018). Food banks need not be a public sector responsibility, but may be a private initiative from, for example, different NGOs.

Access to health, including the ability to get necessary medicine, can further be an issue. A persistently low income then, if there are user charges connected to the use of healthcare and/or purchasing medicine, might reduce poor people's access to necessary (or early) treatment when they are in need. This contributes to the anxiety felt by the poorest people's daily lives.

There are a number of in-kind services that can be important for those living in or at risk of poverty. Even if they are available in a country with low economic growth, the living standard for poor people is at least slightly better.

5.4.3 FINANCING AND POVERTY

How the financing of welfare states influences poverty depends both on how taxes and duties are managed, and also on the way the actual system is structured. Overall, it seems that taxes and duties are less effective than social transfers in reducing poverty (Caminada et al. 2019), given that in most tax systems low-income earners will have reduced their take-home income due to the payment of income tax and/or social security contributions. The negative impact on poverty is due to the fact that the calculation includes only how the payment of taxes (and does not include duties) has an impact on the disposable income used to calculate the degree of relative poverty. For those living in absolute poverty this might not be the same, as they have such a low income that they do not have to pay income tax.[1]

The consequences reflect the fact that in most tax systems, income tax is paid even when the threshold set by the system is low. Social security contributions are additional contributions paid on any income, and thus reduce that available income, which then for some, means that they are considered at risk of poverty. This explains that when looking separately at taxation, this might increase poverty, whereas the way money is spent can then reduce the number of people living in poverty. Thus, discussing the impact of the tax system on economic development in isolation means a risk of reaching a result that could be used to argue in favour of reduction in taxes and duties, despite the fact that these are necessary in order to be able to finance welfare systems.

A question arises in relation to the tax system that, in order to cope with poverty, people work extended hours, i.e. they need to work more to be above the poverty line, which might in principle reduce their well-being, and there are those who might prefer to work and consume less than others (Maniquet and Neumann 2016), thus also pointing to the fact that, in principle, income in itself is not sufficient to inform on quality of life for individuals, see also Chapter 4.

Besides, other parts of the tax and duty system can also influence the risk of living in poverty (Greve 2020), as, for example, value added taxes are more important and influence buying power to a greater degree at the bottom of the income distribution. Duties on energy consumption might also be more difficult to pay for low-income groups, indicating sometimes a conflict between environmental and social issues. Redistribution of income by the use of taxes and duties may increase equality in society generally, but this might not necessarily have the same impact on the number of people living in poverty.

Different kinds of tax credits have been used in the tax system as a way of both giving incentives to take up a job (including low-paid jobs), and being helpful in alleviating the risk of working poor, see Chapter 4 and section 5.4.6, and Hick and Lanau (2019). A risk with regard to poverty reduction is that tax credits will only be available to those who actually have a job. Still, they might help in redressing the possibility of a poverty trap, i.e. that even a small increase in income reduces social benefits so that there is no incentive at all to take up a job.

5.4.4 EDUCATION

A core instrument that can be used to reduce or alleviate poverty at least in a longer time perspective seems to be the use of education. This is because education ensures the accumulation of human capital that means, in most countries, a higher chance of getting a job, and also it might mean a higher income and alleviate the risk of working poor. Higher levels of human capital can, besides labour market participation, also mean more democratic participation, etc.

This also explains why in some countries, with South American countries being the first, (Arza and Maurizio 2020), the right to certain social benefits, typically family allowances, depends on children in the family having an education. This is a way of ensuring that the next generation of children gain at least some basic skills, and by this have a possible better start later on when they are eligible for the labour market. A common problem is that it can be difficult to depict and measure the impact of education, including which instruments are the most effective (Case 2006).

Education is here thought of in its broadest understanding; however, with a focus on literacy and numeracy being ensured for most people. In developing countries, a first step might thus be to ensure that no one is illiterate and have some basic mathematical and IT understanding.

Given the expected technological developments on the labour market, it might also be important to have further education, and even life-long learning, as also pointed out very early by the EU in a communication in 2001, where on the front page was the following: '"When planning for a year, plant corn. When planning for a decade, plant trees. When planning for life, train and educate people." Chinese proverb: Guanzi (c.645BC)'.[2] Still, the data, at least within the EU, point out that for many, life-long learning has not been reached. Thus, it is not only basic education, but a continued updating of skills that is necessary.

Higher levels of education in general make it possible to help in using new knowledge, to make new interventions and be on a higher level in the global production process. This also includes the fact that there is a need to support people in returning to education (Macmillan et al. 2018), and labour market policy has a role to play here, see also the next section.

5.4.5 LABOUR MARKET POLICY

Given that having a job is not always a sufficient route to avoid poverty (see in-work poverty in Chapter 4), labour market policy can be an important component. The ability to move jobs from the informal economy to the formal economy can also be considered an important element in the way societies can reduce poverty. This is because jobs in the informal economy are often low paid and with fewer guarantees than those in the formal economy. Ways to reduce the informal economy could thereby also be part of a strategy to reduce poverty, although in parts of the world the informal economy is so large that this would be difficult to achieve.

Overall, labour market policy with a focus on employability can be an important aspect of making life better for people. This ranges from education, see section 5.4.4, but also to further and life-long learning as aspects necessary in a world where labour markets are changing rapidly as a consequence of technological development (Ford 2015; Greve 2017b; Peralta-Alva and Roitman 2018). Thus, those who have not been able to move from one kind of job to another might have a higher risk of ending up living in poverty, especially in countries that do not have generous social income transfers. Thus, the risk of becoming unemployed and living in poverty is overall higher in liberal welfare states than in Nordic welfare states.

Labour market policies can also have the aim of supporting those who have difficulties in getting a permanent job to have better access to the labour market. This can include wage subsidies, but also different kinds of placements and supported employment. For a more detailed presentation of possible elements, see Greve (2018), and for a discussion of the effectiveness of integrating people into the labour market, see Card, Kluve and Weber (2018). Programmes are, unfortunately, not as effective as one could wish. The overall economic development and change in human capital seem, therefore, more generally to be important issues.

Parts of some labour market policies might also be using the minimum wage as a way of protecting workers, even though not always protecting all people on the labour market. It seems at least to have been working in Australia, where it is argued that the 'wage-setting system since its inception has been to protect workers against poverty' (Saunders and Bedford 2018, 282).

In many countries, actors in the labour market also have a role in ensuring good working conditions, including wage income so that working poverty can be reduced and increased health and safety initiatives deployed to prevent accidents so that people are able to continue to work.

5.4.6 OTHER INSTRUMENTS

Helping those below the poverty line does not necessarily depend on direct public sector spending, there might also be the option to impose rules and regulations to improve living standards. Legal approaches cannot be directly found in spending on social protection but might still have an impact on the number of people living in or at risk of poverty.

Direct legal influences include, for example, legislation regarding the minimum wage. Minimum wages on the labour market might help those on the labour market to avoid being working poor, see Chapter 4. Naturally, this might not help on the informal labour market, but it can be a way to help those in the formal labour market. Increases in the minimum wage might keep some from falling below the poverty line. This can be done by, for example, relating the size of the minimum income to reference budgets, which illustrate what can be deemed necessary for avoidance of poverty (Deeming 2017). There is still debate about whether a higher minimum income might mean that some will not be able to get a job. Still, this could also be the case even without a minimum income. It is the case that many developed countries have legislation on minimum income as a way of protecting workers on the labour market, especially in countries where trade unions are not strong and/or there are only a few collective agreements covering a small part of the labour market. Overall, it seems that minimum wage regulations matter, at least for immigrants (Eugster 2018), albeit changes herein might imply that the employers then change other parts of the work conditions for the employed.

Besides regulation of the minimum wage level, in the UK, there are Voluntary Living Wage employers, who promise to pay a minimum wage based upon a calculated basic cost of living (Swaffield et al. 2018). One could argue that this is in line with at least the historical understanding of absolute poverty, see Chapter 2.

Another example is the regulation of the cost of housing. Rent controls may be an effective means of helping those below or close to the poverty line. This is because even those having a very low income have their living standards influenced by what they have to pay for accommodation, food and transport. Economic state support, besides regulation, for lowering prices on necessities for the poor might thus also be a way.

Naturally, there is also the option to support, in different ways, civil society's ability to help those living in poverty, this might include various types of indirect support through the tax system, for example, a reduction in income tax if supporting people in need.

Using redistribution through the tax system by tax allowances and tax credits does not seem to have a positive impact on poverty, and might even increase the degree of inequality (Avram 2018). The implication is that the role of the tax system to alleviate poverty will function best if it provides enough revenue to finance different kinds of benefits and services.

Lastly, it can be argued that using behavioural knowledge to 'nudge' people to alter their behaviour might reduce poverty given that people do not always act in a rational way, for example, by ill-advisedly taking out loans at a very high rate of interest. Naturally, one needs to be aware of the ethical issues involved, as it is not necessarily sufficient to use 'nudge' because not all might follow advice and seek change, but it might complement state intervention (Curchin 2017).

5.5 TARGET OR NOT TARGETED BENEFITS?

Historically, it has been argued that targeted benefits towards the poorer part of the population might not reduce poverty as effectively as broader approaches to poverty (Korpi and Palme 1998). The argument is that if targeted, there would be less support for higher levels of benefits thereby the ability to lift a number of people out of poverty would be lower than it otherwise might.

Different analysis implies that, seemingly, a paradox still exists, so that higher-spending welfare states reduce poverty more than lower-spending welfare states (Brady and Bostic 2015; Jacques and Noël 2018), see also for Europe, Figure 3.1. A higher level of spending also implies an option for less stringent conditionality attached to those receiving benefits, and it might even make it possible to pay higher benefits than otherwise would be the case. However, it has also been argued that this is not so generally, and the analysis will be highly dependent on the choice of data (Marx, Salanauskaite and Verbist 2013) So, perhaps the question is not whether benefits are targeted or not, but the priority given in each country to resources for welfare purposes and whether they mainly are used for those in need of receiving income benefits. This reflects a difficult balance between helping those most in need, thereby ensuring legitimacy for welfare states, and a system not being very complicated and thereby presumably also supporting more than those most in need.

The issue of legitimacy also influences people's willingness to support those living in poverty, and thereby also people's perception about whether people use or abuse the system. Table 5.1 shows the relation between possible intended and unintended consequence of benefits.

The different perceptions of legitimacy in Table 5.1 might also influence the opinions about whether benefits should be more or less targeted. This does not inform about whether people actually take up

Table 5.1 Perceptions of underuse and overuse of benefits

	Underuse	Overuse
Intended	So, low levels of benefits or strong stigma attached that people do not apply, or difficult administrative procedures so people do not get them	Reflects that if individual gets a benefit they should not have had (fraud or abuse)
Unintended	People do not receive benefits they are eligible to	People not seen as deserving receiving benefits

Source: Inspired by Roosma, van Oorschot and Gelissen (2016).

the benefit they are eligible to, nor whether people know the actual level of the benefits people are entitled to.

The risk with very targeted benefits to those most in need is that their ability to get the benefits can be limited. This might, as an example, be the case for homeless people. So, even in systems with benefits available, it is not necessarily the case that all people get the benefits they are entitled to. Take-up of benefits can thus also be an issue in how to alleviate poverty.

5.6 SUMMING UP

The choice of instruments can have an impact on the number of people living in or at risk of poverty. Besides the choice of instruments, the generosity and conditions attached to the specific benefits also have an impact on the degree of poverty, and the ability to reduce the level of deprivation when using income transfers in particular. Thereby the overall size of welfare states has an impact on the degree of poverty they are able to relieve across different countries.

The impact of the tax system, if analysed separately, is less clear, as this might reduce disposable income for those at risk of poverty, while the spending possible by ensuring a sufficient financing at the same time can reduce the level of poverty. Labour market policy can also be an important issue.

It seems that, not only what can be labelled more traditional welfare state initiatives in relation to income benefits and welfare services, but also the question about the functioning of the educational system influence not only today, but also in the future, the number in or at risk of poverty. Thus educational policy matter.

NOTES

1 The study referred to is for developed countries.
2 From www.europarl.europa.eu/meetdocs/committees/cult/20020122/com(2001) 678_en.pdf, accessed 27 March 2019.

REFERENCES

Addison, Tony, David Hulme and Ravi Kanbur. 2009. *Poverty Dynamics: Interdisciplinary Perspectives*. Oxford: Oxford University Press.

Alkire, Sabina, José Manuel Roche, Paola Ballon, James Foster, Maria Emma Santos and Suman Seth. 2015. *Multidimensional Poverty Measurement and Analysis*. New York: Oxford University Press.

Arza, Camila and Roxana Maurizio. 2020. 'Poverty and Social Policy in Latin America: Key Trends since c. 2000', in Bent Greve (ed.), *The Routledge International Handbook of Poverty*, 1st edn. Abingdon: Routledge.

Avram, Silvia. 2018. 'Who Benefits from the "Hidden Welfare State"? The Distributional Effects of Personal Income Tax Expenditure in Six Countries', *Journal of European Social Policy* 28(3): 271–93. https://doi.org/10.1177/0958928717735061.

Bastagli, Francesca, Jessica Hagen-Zanker, Luke Harman, Valentina Barca, Georgina Sturge and Tanja Schmidt. 2018. 'The Impact of Cash Transfers: A Review of the Evidence from Low- and Middle-Income Countries', *Journal of Social Policy*, 48(3): 569–94. https://doi.org/10.1017/S0047279418000715.

Been, Jim, Koen Caminada, Kees Goudswaard and Olaf Vliet. 2016. 'Public/Private Pension Mix, Income Inequality and Poverty among the Elderly in Europe: An Empirical Analysis Using New and Revised OECD Data', *Social Policy & Administration* 51(7): 1079–1100. https://doi.org/10.1111/spol.12282.

Ben-Ami, Daniel. 2012. *Ferraris for All: In Defence of Economic Progress*. Bristol: Policy Press.

Berghman, Jos, Anneliese Debels and Ine Van Hoyweghen. 2019. 'Prevention: The Cases of Social Security and Healthcare,' in Bent Greve (ed.) *Routledge Handbook of the Welfare State*, 2nd edn. Abingdon: Routledge.

Bradshaw, Jonathan. 2000. 'Preface for the Centennial Edition of Poverty: A Study in Town Life', in Benjamin Seebohm Rowntree and Jonathan Bradshaw (eds) *Poverty: A Study of Town Life*, 1st edn, pp. xix–lxxxii. Bristol: Policy Press.

Brady, David and Amie Bostic. 2015. 'Paradoxes of Social Policy: Welfare Transfers, Relative Poverty, and Redistribution Preferences', *American Sociological Review* 80(2): 268–98. https://doi.org/10.1177/0003122415573049.

Caminada, Koen, Jinxian Wang, Kees Goudswaard and Chen Wang. 2019. 'Relative Income Poverty Rates and Poverty Alleviation via Tax/Benefit Systems in 49 LIS-Countries, 1967–2016', Working Paper No. 761. Luxembourg: LIS Cross-National Data Center.

Card, David, Jochen Kluve and Andrea Weber. 2018. 'What Works? A Meta Analysis of Recent Active Labor Market Program Evaluations', *Journal of the European Economic Association* 16(3): 894–931. https://doi.org/10.1093/jeea/jvx028.

Case, Anne. 2006. 'The Primacy of Education', in Abhikit Vinayak Banerjee, Roland Bénabou and Dilip Mookherjee (eds) *Understanding Poverty*. Oxford: Oxford University Press, pp. 269–85.

Chzhen, Yekaterina and Jonathan Bradshaw. 2012. 'Lone Parents, Poverty and Policy in the European Union', *Journal of European Social Policy* 22(5): 487–506. https://doi.org/10.1177/0958928712456578.

Cournède, Boris, Jean-Marc Fournier and Peter Hoeller. 2018. 'Public Finance Structure and Inclusive Growth', OECD Economic Papers No. 25. Paris: OECD Publishing. https://doi.org/https://doi.org/10.1787/e99683b5-en.

Curchin, Katherine. 2017. 'Using Behavioural Insights to Argue for a Stronger Social Safety Net: Beyond Libertarian Paternalism', *Journal of Social Policy* 46(2): 231–49.

Daly, Mary. 2018. 'Towards a Theorization of the Relationship between Poverty and Family', *Social Policy & Administration* 52(3): 565–77.

Deeming, Christopher and Paul Smyth (eds) 2018. *Reframing Global Social Policy. Social Investment for Sustainable and Inclusive Growth.* Bristol: Policy Press.

Deeming, Christopher. 2017. 'Defining Minimum Income (and Living) Standards in Europe: Methodological Issues and Policy Debates', *Social Policy and Society* 16(1): 33–48.

Eugster, Beatrice. 2018. 'Immigrants and Poverty, and Conditionality of Immigrants' Social Rights', *Journal of European Social Policy* 28(5): 452–70. https://doi.org/10.1177/0958928717753580.

Ford, Martin. 2015. *Rise of the Robots: Technology and the Threat of Mass Unemployment.* New York: Basic Books.

Goedemé, Tim, John Hills and Bea Cantillon. 2019. *Decent Incomes for All: Improving Policies in Europe.* Oxford: Oxford University Press.

Greve, Bent. (ed.) 2017a. *Handbook of Social Policy Evaluation.* Cheltenham: Edward Elgar. https://doi.org/10.4337/9781785363245.

Greve, Bent. 2017b. *Technology and the Future of Work. The Impact on Labour Markets and Welfare States.* Cheltenham: Edward Elgar.

Greve, Bent. 2019. *Welfare Populism and Welfare Chauvinism.* Bristol: Policy Press.

Greve, Bent. (ed.) 2020. *The Routledge International Handbook of Poverty*, 1st edn. Abingdon: Routledge.

Greve, Bent. 2018. *Social and Labour Market Policy: The Basics.* Abingdon: Routledge.

Heckman, James J. 2006. 'Skill Formation and the Economics of Investing in Disadvantaged Children', *Science* 312: 1900–1902.

Hick, Rod and Alba Lanau. 2019. 'Tax Credits and In-Work Poverty in the UK: An Analysis of Income Packages and Anti-Poverty Performance', *Social Policy and Society* 18(2): 219–36.

Jacques, Olivier and Alain Noël. 2018. 'The Case for Welfare State Universalism, or the Lasting Relevance of the Paradox of Redistribution', *Journal of European Social Policy* 28(1): 70–85. https://doi.org/10.1177/0958928717700564.

Jacques, Philippe, Marie-Louise Leroux and Dalibor Stevanovic. 2018. 'Poverty Among the Elderly: The Role of Public Pension Systems', Working paper, No. 18–07. Québec: Cahiers de Recherche.

Jefferson, Philip N. 2020. 'Global Poverty: Trends, Measures, and Antidotes', in Bent Greve (ed.), *The Routledge International Handbook of Poverty*, 1st edn. Abingdon: Routledge.

Korpi, Walter and Joakim Palme. 1998. 'The Paradox of Redistribution and Strategies of Equality: Welfare State Institutions, Inequality and Poverty in the Western Countries', No. 174. Luxembourg: LIS Working Paper Series.

Korpi, Walter and Joakim Palme. 2003. 'New Politics and Class Politics in the Context of Austerity and Globalization: Welfare State Regress in 18 Countries, 1975–95', *American Political Science Review* 97(3): 425–46. https://doi.org/10.1017/S0003055403000789.

Lambie-Mumford, Hannah. 2019. 'The Growth of Food Banks in Britain and What They Mean for Social Policy', *Critical Social Policy* 39(1): 3–22.

Leiser, David and Yhonatan Shemesh. 2018. *How We Misunderstand Economics and Why It Matters: The Psychology of Bias, Distortion and Conspiracy*. Abingdon: Routledge.

Leisering, Lutz 2020. 'Social Cash Transfers in the Global South: Individualizing Poverty Policies', in Bent Greve (ed.), *The Routledge International Handbook of Poverty*, 1st edn. Abingdon: Routledge.

Leventi, Chrysa, Holly Sutherland and Iva Valentinova Tasseva. 2017. 'Improving Poverty Reduction in Europe: What Works (Best) Where?', *EUROMOD Working Paper Series*, EM 8/17. https://doi.org/10.1177/0958928718792130.

Macmillan, Lindsay, Paul Gregg, John Jerrim and Nikki Shure. 2018. 'Children in Jobless Households across Europe: Evidence on the Association with Medium- and Long-Term Outcomes', *Journal of Poverty and Social Justice* 26(3): 335–58.

Maniquet, François and Dirk Neumann. 2016. 'Well-Being, Poverty and Labor Income Taxation: Theory and Application to Europe and the US', Center for Operations Research and Econometrics (CORE), Discussion Papers, No. 2016029. Louvain: Université catholique de Louvain.

Marx, Ive, Lina Salanauskaite, and Gerlinde Verbist. 2013. 'The Paradox of Redistribution Revisited: And That It May Rest in Peace?', IZA DP No. 7414. Bonn: IZA.

Middleton, Georgia, Kaye Mehta, Darlene McNaughton and Sue Booth. 2018. 'The Experiences and Perceptions of Food Banks amongst Users in High-Income Countries: An International Scoping Review', *Appetite* 120:698–708.

Murray, Charles A. and Frank Field. 1990. *The Emerging British Underclass*. London: IEA Health and Welfare Unit.

OECD. 2015. *In It Together: Why Less Inequality Benefits All.* Paris: OECD Publishing.

Oorschot, Wim van. 2006. 'Making the Difference in Social Europe: Deservingness Perceptions among Citizens of European Welfare States', *Journal of European Social Policy* 16(1): 23–42. https://doi.org/10.1177/0958928706059829.

Peralta-Alva, Adrian and Agustin Roitman. 2018. 'Technology and the Future of Work', WP/18/207. IMF Working Paper, 28pp.

Purdam, Kingsley, Elisabeth A. Garratt and Aneez Esmail. 2016. 'Hungry? Food Insecurity, Social Stigma and Embarrassment in the UK', *Sociology* 50(6): 1072–88. http://10.0.4.153/0038038515594092.

Romano, Serena. 2017. *Moralising Poverty: The 'Undeserving' Poor in the Public Gaze.* Abingdon: Routledge.

Roosma, Femke, Wim van Oorschot and John Gelissen. 'A Just Distribution of Burdens? Attitudes Toward the Social Distribution of Taxes in 26 Welfare States', *International Journal of Public Opinion Research* 28(3): 376–400.

Saltkjel, Therese and Ira Malmberg-Heimonen. 2017. 'Welfare Generosity in Europe: A Multi-Level Study of Material Deprivation and Income Poverty among Disadvantaged Groups', *Social Policy and Administration* 51(7): 1287–1310. https://doi.org/10.1111/spol.12217.

Saunders, Peter and Megan Bedford. 2018. 'New Minimum Healthy Living Budget Standards for Low-Paid and Unemployed Australians', *The Economic and Labour Relations Review* 29(3): 273–88.

Sinfield, Adrian 2020. 'Preventing Poverty', in Bent Greve (ed.), *The Routledge International Handbook of Poverty*, 1st edn. Abingdon: Routledge.

Swaffield, Jo, Carolyn Snell, Becky Tunstall and Jonathan Bradshaw. 2018. 'An Evaluation of the Living Wage: Identifying Pathways Out of In-Work Poverty', *Social Policy and Society* 17(3): 379–92.

Taylor-Gooby, Peter, Julia M. Gumy and Adeline Otto. 2015. 'Can "New Welfare" Address Poverty through More and Better Jobs?', *Journal of Social Policy* 44(1): 83–104. https://doi.org/10.1017/S0047279414000403.

Vliet, Olaf van, Koen Caminada, Kees Goudswaard, and Jinxuan Wang. 2020. 'Poverty Reduction Mog Older People through Pensions: A Comparative Analysis', in Bent Greve (ed.), *The Routledge International Handbook of Poverty*, 1st edn. Abingdon: Routledge.

Will, Jeffry A. 1993. 'The Dimensions of Poverty: Public Perceptions of the Deserving Poor', *Social Science Research* 22(1): 312–32. https://doi.org/10.1006/ssre.1993.1016.

INTERNATIONAL PERSPECTIVES ON POVERTY

6.1 INTRODUCTION

Over the years, there has been strong international collaboration in relation to poverty. This chapter starts, in section 6.2, with a focus on the UN's Sustainable Development Goals (SDGs) and the goal of eradicating extreme poverty and then presents the international collaboration in relation to poverty, including organisations such as UNICEF, the World Bank, the OECD and the EU. This is followed by a presentation on poverty and its relation to migration (section 6.3), while transfers from rich to poor countries and international support for development, mainly in less developed countries, are the focus of section 6.4. It will be seen that transfers are not only economic, but also of knowledge – a further way of reducing poverty internationally. Section 6.5 then looks into the relation between technological developments, which might move production around the globe to as well as away from countries with an abundant number of workers. Historically, the movement of jobs towards low-income countries in industrial production might be weaker in the years to come. This section also touches upon economic growth as one way, but not the only way, that might help in the alleviation of poverty, although this will depend on the way in which economic growth is distributed. The recent years' rise in economic inequality around the globe indicates that it is also a question of how resources are distributed in different countries.

6.2 INTERNATIONAL ORGANISATIONS AND POVERTY

There are many and varied international organisations with interest, knowledge and information related to poverty. Besides international organisations, in individual countries there might be available information including both quantitative data and qualitative analysis related to their activities. Agenda setting and information are central instruments that can be used by these international organisations in order to help in reducing the level of poverty. This also includes the goals, see more in section 6.4, of what is expected of the richer countries to transfer to the poorer countries. Besides agenda setting and information, there are a number of international organisations supporting people in need in the different countries. There can also be national NGOs supporting the development, often financed by external donors. Even if they can have an important role, the focus here is on the large international organisations with information and analysis of the situation. The section does not look into the possible effectiveness of the use of money, but one needs to try as best as possible to find projects where there is evidence that this can help in reducing the level of poverty.

First and foremost, as already pointed out in Chapter 1, there is the UN's target of eradicating extreme poverty by 2030. The reason why this is important is that the UN is an international organisation with worldwide member countries, including countries with developing and emerging economies. Although the UN is not able to demand for example, monetary transfer and support to those living in poverty, it can by setting goals, alert us to the consequences of poverty, create dialogue between states and exert pressure on different countries in the effort to act on poverty. The UN includes a number of organisations and agencies with different purposes and options with regard to poverty.

The UNDP (United Nations Development Programme) works in more than 170 countries with different projects and the aim of helping in alleviating poverty.[1] There is a food programme (World Food Programme), an organisation dealing with labour standards (ILO – International Labour Organization) and the International

Monetary Fund (IMF) focusing on supporting countries in economic development.

The ILO website states: 'The only tripartite U.N. agency, since 1919 the ILO brings together governments, employers and workers of 187 member states, to set labour standards, develop policies and devise programmes promoting decent work for all women and men.'[2]

Promoting decent work can help to avoid poverty as it includes also decent social protection. The ILO's website contains information on wages, social protection, etc. That it is a tripartite body implies an attempt to include all central actors related to labour markets, which is important given the importance of the labour market for the risk of or living in poverty.

One of the larger organisations in relation to poverty is UNICEF. This is an organisation that does the following 'UNICEF works in 190 countries and territories to save children's lives, to defend their rights, and to help them fulfil their potential, from early childhood through adolescence. And we never give up'.[3]

This therefore also includes a focus on poverty and information is published regularly on the numbers, especially children, living in poverty and the impact of this[4] in a number of different ways, including on the multidimensional understanding of poverty. UNICEF's projects also include elements that help in protecting children's upbringing, see more on its website at www.unicef.org/socialpolicy/index_childpoverty.html.

Another large UN organisation is the World Health Organization (WHO) that: 'works worldwide to promote health, keep the world safe, and serve the vulnerable'.[5] Given that those living in poverty have a higher risk of poor health, including the risk of diseases related to not having shelter, clean water, etc., this is important. The way in which the WHO supports those at risk is therefore also a way to inform on poverty. In addition, statistics are provided with information on health status, different kind of diseases, etc. This information is available for a number of countries and can thereby help to paint a picture of the situation that in many ways is directly related to the consequence of living standards and the degree of poverty in different countries, for example, life expectancy is higher in countries with lower levels of poverty.

The World Bank, established in 1944, aims to support developing countries, with 189 member countries involved in activities and projects in relation to poverty across the globe. The World Bank describes its activities as follows:

> Today the Bank Group's work touches nearly every sector that is important to fighting poverty, supporting economic growth, and ensuring sustainable gains in the quality of people's lives in developing countries. While sound project selection and design remain paramount, the Bank Group recognises a wide range of factors that are critical to success— effective institutions, sound policies, continuous learning through evaluation and knowledge-sharing, and partnership, including with the private sector. The Bank Group has long-standing relationships with more than 180 member countries, and it taps these to address development challenges that are increasingly global.
>
> (World Bank 2017)[6]

There are many and varied data in relation to poverty available on the World Bank website, as well as descriptions of different kind of projects with the aim of ensuring positive development. As acknowledged in the quote above, projects are not always successful and there can be many and varied risks and hindrances for the development of these different projects.

The EU has for a long time focused on the necessity of reducing poverty in order to make Europe function more effectively. In July 1975, the European Council agreed the first relative definition of poverty and at the same time the first programmes to combat poverty was issued. Furthermore, the Lisbon Summit in 2000 stated that the number of people living in poverty was unacceptable (Urquijo 2017).

Fighting poverty was included in the Open Method of Co-ordination (OMC) (Hermann 2017); however, the EU does not formally have competence to do anything, as this is the responsibility of nation states. Only if there are rules related to the free movement of workers and gender equality might there be some supranational competences. Recommendations within the OMC related to poverty have been limited, with 2013 as an exception, as shown in an analysis of recommendations from 2011 to 2015 (Urquijo 2017, 55).

In 2010, the EU set a target that by 2020, 20 million people should be lifted out of poverty,[7] although in 2016 it was less than 10 million, so it seems that the goal will not be reached. Still, it is an indicator that by setting an agenda, international organisations might over time have an impact on the goal of alleviating, or at least reducing, poverty, even if they do not have the formal power to make decisions which can achieve the goal.

Other regional associations around the globe also have perspectives and ideas about how to deal with and support economic and social development: The Oxford Poverty and Human Development Initiative (OPHI), informs about development and publishes research reports, see for the latest report https://ophi.org.uk/multidimensional-poverty-index/global-mpi-2018/. There is also a site with reports on the situation in 105 developing countries, https://ophi.org.uk/multidimensional-poverty-index/mpi-country-briefings/, and information on various countries can be found here, which are beyond the scope of this book.

6.3 MIGRATION AND POVERTY

In 2015, there were more than 150 million migrant workers globally and in total more than 250 million international migrants.

Migration and poverty is by no means a simple and one-directional issue. It includes a number of different perspectives and is an area where the knowledge on the number of people living in poverty due to migration might be less clear. This is because migration is caused by a number of reasons and for very different reasons, such as availability of work (Greve 2012). There are both push and pull factors and international migration has partly been seen as 'brain drain' from emerging and developing countries. It can also be due to poverty, such as the high level of poverty in Sub-Saharan Africa, which means that some, at least, are willing to risk a great deal in their efforts to migrate. Whether this is the case overall can be questioned, albeit the many news articles related to people trying to cross the Mediteranean is a strong indicator hereof. There might also be other issues at stake (Sener 2020).

There can be an impact on poverty in both the sending and the receiving countries. In sending countries, if the poor migrate then this could, in principle, reduce poverty, especially if they are able to send money home, see also section 6.4. However, if those migrating possess high levels of education, the country risks depletion of a highly skilled labour force. Financial support provided by this group of migrants certainly alleviates the number of people living in poverty in the sending countries.

For receiving countries, the question is in a number of ways the opposite. There can be four different types of impact. These include the impact on wages on the labour market and the cost of commodities, public services and finances, although the overall impact of these four elements is difficult to estimate, it seems, at least for the UK, to be limited (Vargas-Silva, Markaki and Sumption 2016).

Looking first at the impact on the labour market, this can be dependent on the level of migrant qualifications. If those migrating have competences which are needed on the labour market and they get a job, then it might help in the overall development of this society by increasing production and reducing pressure on the labour market. The overall impact then depends on the size of remittances. If migrants are low-skilled, this might cause a pressure on the wages of those with already low incomes, thereby with a risk of more working poor, or some losing their jobs. Wage effects seem to be the largest for migrants already living in the receiving country as they are often in a more precarious position on the labour market than natives.

The second issue depends on what happens with the migration. If migration helps in ensuring more production at a lower price, then in principle this should also imply lower prices which could be beneficial for low-income groups.

In relation to public finances and services, there might also be both positive and less positive short as well as long-term impacts. Migrants will often be in less of need of education and use of services as they are often relatively young. It will also depend on the size of benefits to those not able to support themselves and thereby there will be an impact on the way in which welfare states function. If those arriving are working and have limited need for public services, then this could imply better finances, again dependent on whether it means that others lose their jobs.

Still, if those migrating have difficulties being integrated on the labour market, whether due to language, culture, competences or discrimination, then this might mean that they will live in poverty in the receiving country. They might also be in need of support from the welfare state. It seems that the access to benefits and jobs on the labour market, but also minimum wages regulation influence the risk of poverty for immigrants within 19 industrialised countries mainly from Europe, but also including Australia and the US (Eugster 2018).

Overall, data related to migration is not often very precise due to the variety of reasons for migration and often data is mainly available for the OECD area, where the most recent data indicate a yearly inflow of around five million persons into the OECD countries.[8] The impact of poverty on those migrating is dependent on having a job, whether it is in the informal sector or within the traditional labour market. The overall impact also depends on whether an inflow of workers causes pressure, particularly on low-income workers, who as a result, will experience poorer conditions within the labour market.

Whether migration causes overall positive and negative impacts might vary across countries. For sending countries, some of the benefit of remittances and migrants returning with knowledge might be positive. For others, it might cause 'brain drain' and thereby less economic development than otherwise could have been achieved. For receiving countries, it is highly dependent on integration within the labour market.

6.4 TRANSFERS FROM RICH TO POOR COUNTRIES

There are different kind of transfers from rich to poor countries. There is development support from richer countries. There are remittances from those working abroad sent back to their home country as mentioned above. There can also be an impact on direct economic investment to develop production, infrastructure, etc. This is not the place to go into detail about the impacts, including the effectiveness, of foreign direct investment, but as always there might be pros and cons. Pros by creating economic activities and cons by increased dependency on the country investing money.

Remittances are very important for low- and middle-income countries and the level reached $466 billion in 2017,[9] which is three times as large as the official development support. At the country level, the highest levels were received in India ($62.7 billion), China ($61 million) and the Philippines (close to $30 million) (World Bank Group 2017). The figures as a proportion of the overall economy are albeit larger in other countries, with Kyrgyzstan the highest receiver with 34.5 per cent of GDP, followed by Nepal (29.7 per cent) and Liberia (29.6 per cent), indicating that for some economies the remittances are extremely important. Compared to where in the world there are the largest number living in absolute poverty (Sub-Saharan Africa), the total flow to these countries is in fact compared to the total limited at $34 billion in 2017, i.e. below 10 per cent of all remittances. This partly reflects the fact that those migrating from the area might have difficulties in getting employment in the formal economy and also that for some it is not possible to migrate. This is also because it might be costly to migrate.

Internally in some of the countries, the remittances also mean that families receiving them might be better off than those families who do not receive them. This thereby creates new divisions in sending countries, while also being of strong economic importance for these countries. In itself, this difference of living standard in countries between those where persons have migrated and other countries can, in itself, be a driver for others wanting to migrate.

There is also an issue of the transaction cost attached to remittances, as those transferring the money charge for doing so, including the cost of buying and selling different currencies and thus this reduces the value of the money. Therefore, internationally, the aim has been to try to reduce these costs.

There has been for a long time a UN goal that countries should designate at least 0.7 per cent of their GDP to developing countries, with the aim of, among other thing, helping towards economic development, that might also help in reducing the number of people living in poverty. However, only a few countries actually spend this amount of money.[10] This is shown in Figure 6.1.

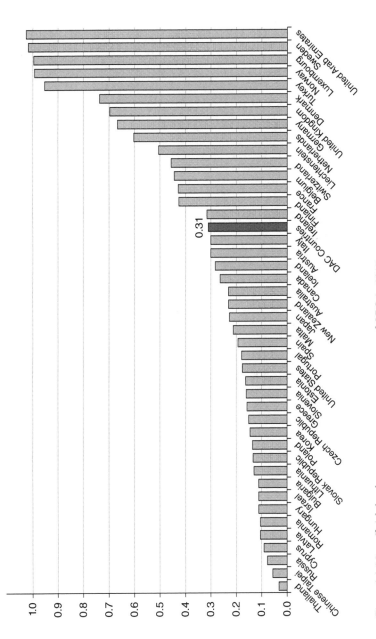

Figure 6.1 Net official development support as percentages of GDP in 2017

Source: Available at https://data.oecd.org/oda/net-oda.htm#indicator-chart, accessed 31 March 2019.

Figure 6.1 shows that the target mainly is reached by Nordic European countries as well as the United Arab Emirates and Turkey. Overall, there is thus still a long way to go to reach the set goal.

6.5 TECHNOLOGY, ECONOMIC DEVELOPMENT AND POVERTY

For many years, industrial production has often been relocated to countries where the labour costs have been lower, causing transfer of jobs from the developed countries to developing countries. The movement of jobs to areas with low labour cost has been a core reason for the relocation of production. However, given that new technology might be more precise and that if, for example, increasingly using robots, which after the initial outlay, do not have any hourly cost attached, this might mean that the same amount of jobs as previously will not be moved to developing countries. There is even the risk that jobs will be moved back, also due to the fact that even if transport costs are low, proximity to the market can mean lower transportation cost.

Thereby, the invention and implementation of new technology can be a reason why poverty will continue to prevail, and that economic development might be more difficult to enact in developing countries than in previous years. New technology might in affluent countries cause new groups of workers to live in poverty dependent on the size of benefits (Greve 2017). This is not to say that the wage cost does not have an impact, but more that the driver of moving jobs to low-wage countries might in the years to come be less strong than it has been in previous years. Emergent economies with growing wage levels can also risk the movement of jobs away from them.

6.6 SUMMING UP

International organisations function as agenda-setters with regard to poverty, and compile and distribute information on the extent and consequences of poverty. In reality, they may lack formal power to enact significant change, albeit a number of projects and varied kinds of support can be found which might help in reducing poverty. Even within the EU, despite the historical emphasis on poverty and having had programmes on poverty for a long time, the relative poverty level is still high and implementing social policies that might do something about the level of poverty is a national issue. Anyhow, it is important to have continued and updated information on poverty and its impact on citizens as this can be the first way to know what can be done.

International organisations are sources of information on migration and the impact thereof. Migration from the Global South to the Global North has been on the agenda for years and that focus is often increased in times of insecurity. Thus, migration can be a reason for both an increase and, also in fact, a decrease in the level of poverty dependent on who is migrating, whether they get good jobs and the amount of remittances they send back home. In more affluent countries in recent years, there has been growing discussion on whether and when to accept migrants. One argument is that it would be better to help people in their home country.

However, international economic support to developing countries is still, for most countries, far from the goal of 0.7 per cent of GDP. Thus, even if there is international economic support, whether effective or not, it is far from the expected international level and therefore too, the possible impact on poverty is perhaps not so strong.

Developments in technology which reduce requirement for cheaper manual labour put further pressure on countries where production has been relocated. Robotics and other manufacturing technologies mean that jobs could be restored to the countries of origin, or at least to countries closer to the market for the products. This might further influence the risk of poverty in affluent countries.

There are still therefore, many international challenges, but also options, with regard to how to cope with poverty in the years to come.

NOTES

1 www.un.org/en/sections/about-un/funds-programmes-specialized-agencies-and-others/index.html, accessed 11 April 2019.
2 www.ilo.org/global/about-the-ilo/lang—en/index.htm accessed 2 May 2019.
3 www.unicef.org/what-we-do, accessed 5 April 2019.

4 See for example, www.unicef-irc.org/publications/pdf/RC13_eng.pdf, accessed 4 April 2019 with information on number of children living in poverty around the globe.
5 www.who.int/about/what-we-do, accessed 11 April 2019.
6 www.worldbank.org/en/about/history, accessed 11 April 2019.
7 See https://ec.europa.eu/eurostat/web/europe-2020-indicators, and https://eur-lex.europa.eu/LexUriServ/LexUriServ.do?uri=COM:2010:2020:FIN:EN:PDF, accessed 5 April 2019.
8 See https://migrationdataportal.org/themes/international-migration-flows, accessed 31 March 2019.
9 https://publications.iom.int/system/files/pdf/global_migration_indicators_2018.pdf, accessed 31 March 2019.
10 https://data.oecd.org/oda/net-oda.htm, accessed 31 March 2019.

REFERENCES

Eugster, Beatrice. 2018. 'Immigrants and Poverty, and Conditionality of Immigrants' Social Rights', *Journal of European Social Policy* 28(5): 452–70. https://doi.org/10.1177/0958928717753580.

Greve, Bent. 2012. 'Labour Migration and Labour Market Integration: Causes and Challenges', in Emma Carmel, Alfio Cerami and Theodoros Papadopoulos (eds), *Migration and Welfare in the New Europe: Social Protection and the Challenges of Integration*. Bristol: Policy Press.

Greve, Bent. 2017. *Technology and the Future of Work: The Impact on Labour Markets and Welfare States*. Cheltenham: Edward Elgar.

Hermann, Christoph. 2017. 'Crisis, Structural Reform and the Dismantling of the European Social Model(s)', *Economic and Industrial Democracy* 38(1): 51–68. https://doi.org/10.1177/0143831X14555708.

Sener, Meltem Yilmaz. 2020. 'International Migration and Poverty', in Bent Greve (ed.), *The Routledge International Handbook of Poverty*, 1st edn. Abingdon: Routledge.

Urquijo, Laura Gómez. 2017. 'The Europeanisation of Policy to Address Poverty under the New Economic Governance: The Contribution of the European Semester', *Journal of Poverty and Social Justice* 25(1): 49–64.

Vargas-Silva, Carlos, Yvonni Markaki and Madeleine Sumption. 2016. Report, 'The Impacts of International Migration on Poverty in the UK', York: Joseph Rowntree Foundation.

World Bank Group. 2017. 'Migration and Remittances. Recent Development and Outlook' Migration and Development Brief No. 27. Washington DC: World Bank Group.

7

CONCLUDING REMARKS

7.1 INTRODUCTION

This last chapter is relatively short and concludes the book by trying to depict possible pathways towards the aim of reducing or even eradicating poverty. This includes a presentation in section 7.2 of a number of successful cases around the globe in reducing the number of people living in poverty. Then, in section 7.3, it draws on historical reasons for poverty reduction as an indicator of what can be done. This is supplemented by a recapitulation of where there is evidence and knowledge of which instruments are available for doing so. Section 7.4 discusses possible barriers to reaching the UN goal of eradicating extreme poverty by 2030 and section 7.5 tries to draw some general lessons from the book.

7.2 EXAMPLES OF SUCCESSFUL POVERTY REDUCTION CASES

As depicted in several of the chapters, there are a variety of ways to reduce the number of people living in poverty, both when measuring it as absolute poverty and relative poverty.

In some countries, minimum income guarantees for jobs on the labour market has been a helpful instrument, as this has helped to reduce the number of people being in a position of working poor. A minimum wage policy has risks, including, at least in theory, that a high level might make it difficult for some people to get a job as the demand at that level might be low for some groups. It also risks increasing the informal economy, which also explains why this kind of policy is mainly found in more developed countries, where the informal labour force is smaller than in developing countries. Thus, also policies reducing the impact of the hidden economy can be seen as an example of a positive impact on the number of people working poor. Regulation of working conditions and improvements in health and safety for workers, can also be understood as a way of preventing poverty by the retention of labour. Sickness and ill-health reduce the possibility of achieving full employment.

Poverty is not only a question of how the market, including the labour market, actually functions. It is also a question of the public policy including the use of instruments that can help to reduce poverty. These range from prevention, for example, by ensuring education for all, which has been the aim of the conditional cash programmes in South America. Long-term reduction of illiteracy should in the future create a better qualified labour force and also that more people might be able to be less dependent on the state.

Education at a high level, without dependence on a social security programme, can overall be seen as a strategy that might reduce poverty, not only now, but also in the future. Those growing up in poverty (Lancker and Vinck 2020; Macmillan et al. 2018) experience disadvantages later in life, including a higher risk of not acquiring a formal education.

If prevention does not work, or other circumstances mean that people end up in poverty, then this overall will also depend on the support from welfare systems in society, including different types of in-kind and in-cash benefits. Given that the risk of living in poverty is often higher for children and the elderly, effective instruments to reduce the numbers of those living in poverty relate to benefits to families and to old-age pensions.

A pension system that ensures a decent living standard for the elderly helps to reduce povery for this section in society. Whether this should be funded or 'pay-as-you-earn' system or a combination of both can be debated but the central issue is that it should also cover those with a more limited work record, for example people with low income and those who have taken time out of the workplace to raise children.

Overall, it still seems to be the case, as discussed historically (Korpi and Palme 1998), that larger welfare states seem better able to help in alleviating poverty, despite the fact that targeting might be less strong. This is in contrast to arguments that one should target benefits to those most in need. Still, both in-cash and in-kind benefits and to some extent working tax credit, can be useful ways of reducing the number of people living in poverty.

7.3 HISTORICAL REASONS FOR REDUCTION IN POVERTY

Looking at absolute poverty, the strongest impact on numbers has been economic growth, especially in large countries such as China and India. This is a strong indicator that economic development is, if the gain from economic growth is at least somehow distributed within a society, a way to reduce poverty. Whether continued economic growth is compatible with climate change is not the focus of this book, but even so, there is still the question on why those living in countries with high levels of absolute poverty should not have the opportunity to raise their standard of living (Ben-Ami 2012).

Growing economic development will most likely also cause a growth in the number of jobs and job creation in the formal economy can be a means to reduce poverty. This is because new jobs in the informal sector do not to the same extent help in reducing poverty, because this (as shown in Chapter 5) implies that more people are in the category of working poor.

Growing economic development will, in fact, not only mean jobs for those in the sectors producing new goods and services, but often also in other sectors of the economy as more people are able to buy a larger variety of goods and services.

Part of the reasons for poverty in some countries is civil war and/ or war against neighbouring states. Thus, if a region is more politically stable, it might also make it possible to spend resources not on military and defence requirements, but on economic development, including social programmes that work towards the reduction of poverty.

Another reason for the development has also been the generally better health and level of education in many countries, these two factors increase the likelihood of helping to increase independence and self-support.

Developments in recent years, in relation to higher levels of inequality in many countries, points in a different direction and in Sub-Saharan Africa, a continuing increase in population numbers has been one reason why the regions has seen an increase in poverty.

Naturally, as also shown in section 7.2, development in a number of welfare states of a poverty-alleviating mechanism, including benefits in-kind and in-cash, has helped in reducing the relative level of income poverty. Thus, welfare states' ability to finance and develop programmes also influence the extent of poverty and the ability to reduce poverty.

It is further the case that growth in the number of jobs is important, but also that income is fairly distributed within households and is combined with a well-designed social policy system, including the ability to smooth income losses in times of unemployment (Goedemé, Hills and Cantillon 2019).

7.4 CAN WE REACH THE UN GOAL?

There is still a long way to go to reach the UN goal of eradicating extreme poverty by 2030. Whether to reach the goal, focusing on absolute poverty, is still open for interpretation. It will depend on a number of issues whether the goal can be reached. This reflects both national and international policies, but also global economic development and presumably environmental development too, including the risk of migration due to climate.

In regard to international policies, these are also connected to assistance from the North to the South with economic development and the implementation of systems of poverty reduction, such as education, as previously discussed. So, international economic transfers might be one way of reaching the 2030 goal. Today, only a limited number of countries fulfil the target of transferring 0.7 per cent of GDP to poorer countries. Transfer of resources appears to be especially important to many countries in Sub-Saharan Africa, which is the part of the globe with most people relatively living in absolute poverty.

Reduction of wars, including civil wars, is also a way of supporting development. This is because this could make foreign investment more likely, but political stability allows resources to be allocated for the development of human capital and income transfers to those living in poverty.

In regard to national policies, this requires discussion about whether or not there exists the will and ability to transfer resources aimed at policies that can help those most in need and this could include wider public sector involvement than at the present time.

7.5 CONCLUSION

Academic analysis and political discussion in relation to people living in various degrees of poverty has been undertaken for many years. There is still no agreement about the causes and reasons why poverty exists, ranging from individual to collective explanations. From controllable to uncontrollable, including ill fortune for some, and the occurrence of natural disasters which wipe out family possessions and future opportunities.

As the book has shown, there seem to be variations in the level of poverty which are also dependent on national policies and willingness to do something about the level of poverty. This is because there seem to be policies that might redress the number of people living in poverty – ranging from stable economic development to the use of social benefits, which can be both in-cash or in-kind, that can reduce the level of poverty.

Although data and research inform our knowledge about the extent of poverty, its causes and the range of instruments that can alleviate it, it is however, policy decisions that can, in practice, do something effective to eliminate it.

REFERENCES

Ben-Ami, Daniel. 2012. *Ferraris for All: In Defence of Economic Progress*. Bristol: Policy Press.

Goedemé, Tim, John Hills and Bea Cantillon. 2019. *Decent Incomes for All: Improving Policies in Europe*. Oxford: Oxford University Press.

Korpi, Walter and Joakim Palme. 1998. 'The Paradox of Redistribution and Strategies of Equality: Welfare State Institutions, Inequality and Poverty in the Western Countries', No. 174. Luxembourg: LIS Working Paper Series.

Lancker, Wim Van and Julie Vinck. 2020. 'The Consequence of Growing up Poor', in Bent Greve, (ed.), *The Routledge International Handbook of Poverty*, 1st edn. Abingdon: Routledge.

Macmillan, Lindsay, Paul Gregg, John Jerrim and Nikki Shure. 2018. 'Children in Jobless Households across Europe: Evidence on the Association with Medium- and Long-Term Outcomes', *Journal of Poverty and Social Justice* 26(3): 335–58.

INDEX

References to figures are in *italics*, references to tables in **bold** and references to boxes in ***bold italics***.

absolute poverty: concept and issues 4, 9, ***12***, 15; and economic growth 71, 103; equivalence scale and family size 14; international absolute poverty line 13–14; measuring 12–16; in New Zealand and Australia 42; and poverty development 36; reduction in 2–3, *3*, 5, 15–16, 36–37, **37**, 47, 48; statistics (2015) 15–16, **15**; statistics on children 55; in Sub-Saharan Africa **15**, 16, 36, **37**, 43, 44, 48, 105; and UN goal of eradicating extreme poverty 104; and Voluntary Living Wage (UK) 81

abuse, and poverty 54

Afghanistan, happiness levels **63**

Africa: absolute poverty 15; informal employment 58; poverty development 44; *see also* North Africa; Sub-Saharan Africa

aid *see* development support

amenities: as in-kind benefit 76; *see also* energy consumption

Anand, Sudhir 21

Asia: absolute poverty 4; poverty reduction 44–46; rural poverty 45–46; *see also* Central Asia; East Asia; South Asia

'at risk' of in-work poverty 58–60, **59**

'at risk' of poverty 16–18, **17**, **18**, 25–26, *26*, 39, **40**, 41, 95

Atkinson, Tony 53

Australia: absolute poverty 42; migrant workers and risk of poverty 95; minimum wage 80; net official development support as percentages of GDP (2017) *97*; old age poverty 60; poverty gap *20*; relative poverty development 42; relative poverty rates **19**

Austria: 'at risk' of in-work poverty **59**; 'at risk' of poverty **40**; net official development support as percentages of GDP (2017) *97*; poverty gap *20*

Baltic countries *see* Estonia; Latvia; Lithuania
'basket of goods' ('necessary goods') concept 13, 14
Bedford, Megan 80
Belgium: 'at risk' of in-work poverty **59**; 'at risk' of poverty **40**; net official development support as percentages of GDP (2017) *97*; poverty gap *20*, 21
benefits: and economic growth 72; in-cash benefits 42, 60, 72, 73–75, 83, 102, 104, 105; in-kind benefits 42, 60, 72, 75–76, 83, 102, 104, 105; and in-work poverty 57, 60; perceptions of underuse and overuse of **82**; and relative poverty development 39, 41, 42; targeted vs not targeted benefits 81–83, 103; *see also* welfare states
better life index (OECD) 62
bogus self-employment 58
brain drain 93, 94, 95
Brazil, conditional cash transfers (CCTs) 47
Bulgaria: 'at risk' of in-work poverty **59**; 'at risk' of poverty **40**; net official development support as percentages of GDP (2017) *97*
Burkina Faso, multidimensional poverty 24
Burundi, absolute poverty 15

Canada: net official development support as percentages of GDP (2017) *97*; poverty gap *20*; relative poverty development 41; relative poverty rates **19**
Caribbean, absolute poverty statistics **15**, **37**
cash benefits *see* in-cash benefits

Causa, Orsetta 43
Central African Republic: absolute poverty 15; happiness levels **63**
Central Asia, absolute poverty statistics **15**, 36, **37**
Chad, multidimensional poverty 24
children: 'at risk' of poverty 39, **40**, 41; child benefits 74–75, 102; child maintenance support 56; child poverty in United States 41–42, 56; childcare as in-kind benefit 75; and conditional cash transfers (CCTs) 47; impact of poverty on 55–56, 57; and in-work poverty 63; and multidimensional poverty 24; preventing child poverty 71; *see also* education; UNICEF
Chile: absolute poverty 47; pension reforms and poverty 48; poverty gap *20*
China: Dibao system 45–46; poverty reduction 2, 37, 45, 48, 103; remittances 96
civil society, and support for those in need 69, 81
climate change 44, 103, 104
Colombia, poverty reduction 48
conditional cash transfers (CCTs) 47–48, 73, 102
conflicts/wars, and poverty 70, 103–104, 105
Congo *see* Democratic Republic of Congo
Costa Rica, poverty gap *20*
crime, and poverty 54
Croatia: 'at risk' of in-work poverty **59**; 'at risk' of poverty **40**
Cuba, conditional cash transfers (CCTs) 47
Cyprus: 'at risk' of in-work poverty **59**; 'at risk' of poverty **40**; net official development support as percentages of GDP (2017) *97*
Czech Republic: 'at risk' of in-work poverty **59**; 'at risk' of poverty **40**;

net official development support as percentages of GDP (2017) *97*; poverty gap *20*

data: and absolute poverty measurement 14; on migration 95; and multidimensional poverty 22, 24; at national levels 90; and poverty measurement 4, 10, 30; and preventing poverty 71; UNICEF data 43, 55; World Bank data 43

democratic participation: and human capital 78; and people in poverty 29, 54

Democratic Republic of Congo, absolute poverty 15

Denmark: 'at risk' of in-work poverty **59**; 'at risk' of poverty 39, **40**; happiness levels **63**; net official development support as percentages of GDP (2017) *97*; poverty gap *20*

deprivation *see* material deprivation

deserving vs undeserving poor 12, 69

developed countries: relative poverty 3, 10; technology's impact on labour market 98, 99; *see also* development support; welfare states

developing countries: absolute poverty 13; informal labour market 58; poverty development 36, 43–48; technology's impact on labour market 98, 99; *see also* development support; Global South; remittances

Development Assistance Committee (DAC) countries: net official development support as percentages of GDP (2017) *97*; *see also* OECD (Organisation for Economic Co-operation and Development)

development support 95, 96, 99, 104–105; net official development support as percentages of GDP (2017) *97*

disability, and poverty 28

donations 7, 90; *see also* development support

duties, and reducing poverty 76, 77

East Asia, absolute poverty statistics **15, 37**

Easterlin, Richard A., Easterlin paradox 62

economic growth: and inequality 72; and preventing poverty 71; and reduction in absolute poverty 103–104; and social protection 72

economic transfers *see* development support

education: and economic growth 104; further education 78, 79; life-long learning 78, 79; literacy 78, 102; numeracy 78; and poverty 54, 55, 56, 63, 69, 70; and preventing poverty 71, 72, 102; and reduction of poverty 72, 78–79, 83

El Salvador, absolute poverty 47

the elderly: 'at risk' of poverty 39, **40**, 43; pensions 48, 74, 102–103; poverty in old age 60–61, 63

Elizabeth I, Queen of England, and deserving vs underserving poor 69

energy consumption: duties on 77; *see also* amenities

England: Poor Laws (1388) 12; *see also* United Kingdom (UK)

equivalence scale: and absolute poverty measurement 14; and family structure 69; and multidimensional poverty measurement 24

Estonia: 'at risk' of in-work poverty **59**; 'at risk' of poverty 39, **40**; in-work poverty 41; net official development support as percentages of GDP (2017) *97*; poverty gap *20*

Europe, absolute poverty statistics **15**, 36, **37**

European Union (EU): 'at risk' of
poverty 16–18, **17–18**, 25–26,
26, 39, **40**, 41; 'at risk' of in-work
poverty 58–60, **59**; child benefits
74–75; first programmes to combat
poverty 92, 98; life-long learning
78; Lisbon Summit (2000) on
poverty 92; material deprivation
definition 25; migrant workers and
risk of poverty 95; Open Method of
Co-ordination (OMC) 92; poverty
reduction target 93; relative poverty
development 37, *38*, 39, **40**, 41, 48;
relative poverty line 16–17; social
exclusion 26, *26*; welfare regimes
35–36; *see also* welfare states

family: and absolute poverty
measurement 14–15; intra-household
distribution and poverty 7, 69; and
relative poverty measurement 16;
single parent households 56, 57, 69,
74, 75; and in-work poverty 57
family allowances 74–75, 78
financial crisis (2007): and children
in relative poverty 55; and in-work
poverty 60
financing (of policies aimed at
poverty) 72, 76–78
Finland: 'at risk' of in-work poverty
59; 'at risk' of poverty **40**; happiness
levels **63**; net official development
support as percentages of GDP
(2017) *97*; poverty gap *20*, 21
food banks 76; *see also* World Food
Programme
Forder, Anthony 10
foreign direct investment 95, 105
France: 'at risk' of in-work poverty **59**;
'at risk' of poverty **40**; poverty gap *20*
Franklin, Benjamin 70
further education 78, 79

Germany: 'at risk' of in-work poverty
59; 'at risk' of poverty 39, **40**; net

official development support as
percentages of GDP (2017) *97*;
poverty gap *20*
Global South: in-cash benefits
75; migration from 99; *see also*
developing countries
good governance, and reducing
poverty 73
Greece: 'at risk' of in-work poverty
59, 60; 'at risk' of poverty **40**; net
official development support as
percentages of GDP (2017) *97*;
poverty gap *20*
growth *see* economic growth

Hakovirta, Mia 56
happiness: five most and least happy
nations (2019) **63**; and poverty
62–63, 64
having, loving and being indicators
11, **11**
health: and economic growth 104;
healthcare 70, 76; and poverty
54, 55, 56; *see also* life expectancy;
World Health Organization
(WHO)
Hermansen, Mikkel 43
hidden economy *see* informal labour
market
historical reasons for reduction in
poverty 103–104
Honduras, absolute poverty 47
housing: as in-kind benefit 75–76;
rent controls 81
human capital 54, 71, 78, 80, 105
Hungary: 'at risk' of in-work poverty
59, 60; 'at risk' of poverty **40**; net
official development support as
percentages of GDP (2017) *97*;
poverty gap *20*

Iceland: happiness levels **63**; net official
development support as percentages
of GDP (2017) *97*; poverty gap *20*;
relative poverty rates **19**

ideological perspectives 5, 7–8, 30, 36
in-cash benefits 42, 60, 72, 73–75, 83, 102, 104, 105; *see also* conditional cash transfers (CCTs)
income: and absolute poverty measurement 13–14; 'decent income' notion 41; and relative poverty measurement 16–17; and relative poverty position 27; and the rich 29; *see also* in-work poverty; labour market; wages
India: happiness study 62; multidimensional poverty 24; poverty reduction 2, 37, 45, 46, 48, 103; remittances 96
inequality: in Africa 44; in China 45; and economic/non-economic growth 71, 72; and poverty 10, 28–29, 54, 69, 70; and relative poverty position 27; and tax allowances/tax credits 81; and welfare state 39
informal labour market: and absolute poverty measurement 14; and minimum wage 80, 102; and reducing poverty 79; and in-work poverty 57, 58, 103
in-kind benefits 42, 60, 72, 75–76, 83, 102, 104, 105
international aid *see* development support
International Labour Organization (ILO) 90, 91
International Monetary Fund (IMF) 90–91
international organisations: and reduction of poverty 90–93, 98–99; *see also* European Union (EU); UNICEF; United Nations (UN); United Nations Development Programme (UNDP); World Bank
international perspectives on poverty: chapter overview 6, 89; chapter summary 98–99;

development support 95, 96, *97*; international organisations 90–93; migration and poverty 93–95; remittances 94, 95–96; technology, economic development and poverty 98
investment, foreign direct investment 95, 105
in-work poverty: in affluent welfare states 41; concept and issues 56–60, 63, 68, 69, 71–72; and education 78; EU 'at risk of in-work poverty' figures 58–60, **59**; and informal labour market 57, 58, 103; and minimum wage 80, 101–102; and non-standard employment 43; and taxes 77
Ireland: 'at risk' of in-work poverty **59**; 'at risk' of poverty **40**; net official development support as percentages of GDP (2017) *97*; poverty gap *20*; relative poverty development 39
Israel: net official development support as percentages of GDP (2017) *97*; poverty gap *20*; relative poverty rates 18, **19**
Italy: 'at risk' of in-work poverty **59**, 60; 'at risk' of poverty **40**; net official development support as percentages of GDP (2017) *97*; poverty gap *20*, 21

Japan: net official development support as percentages of GDP (2017) *97*; poverty gap *20*; relative poverty rates **19**, 46, 48
Jefferson, Philip N. 70
Jones, Hayley 47
justice: and poverty 10, 28–29; *see also* inequality

Kane, Emily 41
Korea: net official development support as percentages of GDP

(2017) *97*; poverty gap *20*; relative poverty rates **19**

Kyrgyzstan, remittances 96

labour market: and education, access to 54; informal labour market 14, 57, 58, 79, 80, 102, 103; labour market policy and reducing poverty 79–80, 83; migrant workers' impact on 94–95; part-time work 57–58, 60; and reasons for poverty 68, 69, 71–72; and relative poverty development 39, 41, 43; technology's impact on 98, 99; *see also* income; in-work poverty; wages

Latin America: absolute poverty statistics **15**, **37**, 47; conditional cash transfers (CCTs) 47–48, 73, 102; link between social benefits and education 78, 102; pension reforms and poverty 48; poverty development 47–48

Latvia: 'at risk' of in-work poverty **59**; 'at risk' of poverty 39, **40**; in-work poverty 41; net official development support as percentages of GDP (2017) *97*; poverty gap *20*

legislation: minimum wage 80–81; rent controls 81

Leiser, David 68

Liberia, remittances 96

Liechtenstein, net official development support as percentages of GDP (2017) *97*

life expectancy: and poverty 54, 55, 63, 91; *see also* health

life-long learning 78, 79

literacy 78, 102; *see also* education

Lithuania: 'at risk' of in-work poverty **59**, 60; 'at risk' of poverty 39, **40**; in-work poverty 41; net official development support as percentages of GDP (2017) *97*; poverty gap *20*

Luxembourg: 'at risk' of in-work poverty **59**; 'at risk' of poverty **40**; net official development support as percentages of GDP (2017) *97*; poverty gap *20*

Mackintosh, J. M. 70

macro-economic policies 72

Madagascar, absolute poverty 15

Malta: 'at risk' of in-work poverty **59**, **59**; 'at risk' of poverty **40**; net official development support as percentages of GDP (2017) *97*

marginalisation, and poverty 54

market forces: and neoliberalism 41; and relative poverty development 39

material deprivation: concept 10, *12*; and democratic participation 29; and disability 28; EU definition 25; and in-cash benefits 75; vs monetary poverty 30; and multidimensional poverty 21–22, 24–26, *26*; relative deprivation 27

means-testing 74

measuring poverty: absolute poverty 9, 12–16, *12*; central concepts *12*; chapter overview 3–4; definitions of poverty 10–11; having, loving and being indicators 11, **11**; inequality, justice and poverty 10, 28–29; key issues 9–10; material deprivation 10, *12*; multidimensional poverty 10, 11, *12*, 21–26, *23*; persistent poverty *12*, 14–15; relative poverty 9–10, *12*, 16–21; relative poverty position 10, 11, 27–28; summary 29–30

meso-level policies 72

Mexico: conditional cash transfers (CCTs) 47; poverty gap *20*; relative poverty development 41; relative poverty rates **19**

micro-level policies 72

Middle East: absolute poverty statistics (2015) **15**, **37** migration: and climate change 104; and poverty 93–95, 99; *see also* remittances

minimum wage 57, 80–81, 95, 101–102

monetary poverty 3, 10, 11, 21, 30, 74

MPI (multidimensional poverty index) *see* multidimensional poverty

multidimensional poverty: concept 10, 11, *12*; elements of multidimensional poverty *23*; global statistics (2018) 24; material deprivation 21–22, 24–26, *26*; multidimensional poverty index (MPI) 21, 22–24, 25, 62; 'at risk' of poverty (EU) 25–26, *26*; and UNICEF 91; in United States 42

Murgai, Rinku 46

Narayan, Ambar 46

'necessary goods' ('basket of goods') concept 13, 14

neoliberalism 41

Nepal, remittances 96

Netherlands: 'at risk' of in-work poverty **59**; 'at risk' of poverty 39, **40**; happiness levels **63**; net official development support as percentages of GDP (2017) *97*; poverty gap *20*

New Zealand: absolute poverty 42; net official development support as percentages of GDP (2017) *97*; poverty gap *20*; relative poverty development 42; relative poverty rates **19**

NGOs (non-governmental organisations) 76, 90

Niger, multidimensional poverty 24

North Africa, absolute poverty statistics (2015) **15**, 37

Norway: happiness levels **63**; net official development support as percentages of GDP (2017) *97*; poverty gap *20*; relative poverty rates 18, **19**

nudge theory 81

numeracy 78; *see also* education

OECD (Organisation for Economic Co-operation and Development): better life index 62; migration data 95; old age poverty 60, 61; poverty gap figures (2017) 18, *20*, 21; poverty gap/rates definitions *19*; poverty rates (in non-EU countries, 2014–16) 18, **19**; relative poverty development 43; *see also* Development Assistance Committee (DAC) countries

older people *see* the elderly

the "one per cent" 29

own-account workers 58

Oxford Poverty and Human Development Initiative (OPHI) 93

Pac, Jessica 41–42

Pacific region, absolute poverty statistics **15**, **37**

part-time work, and in-work poverty 57–58, 60

Paul, St, and deserving vs undeserving poor 69

pensions: and reducing poverty 74, 102–103; reforms of in Latin America 48; in welfare states 61

persistent poverty: and absolute poverty measurement 14–15; concept *12*

philanthropy 7, 69

Philippines, remittances 96

platform economy 57–58

Poland: 'at risk' of in-work poverty **59**; 'at risk' of poverty **40**; net official development support as percentages of GDP (2017) *97*; poverty gap *20*

policies aimed at poverty: chapter overview 5–6, 67–68; chapter summary 83; education 72, 78–79; factors of poverty 68–70;

financing of policies 72, 76–78; in-cash benefits 72, 73–75; in-kind benefits 72, 75–76; labour market policy 79–80; legislation 80–81; macro/meso/micro-level policies 72; preventing poverty 70–72; successful poverty reduction cases 101–103, 105; targeted vs not targeted benefits 81–83, **82**

Poor Laws (England, 1388) 12

Portugal: 'at risk' of in-work poverty **59**, 60; 'at risk' of poverty **40**; net official development support as percentages of GDP (2017) *97*; poverty gap *20*

poverty: aim of book 1–2; central concepts *12*; current situation 2–3; definitions 10–11; deserving vs undeserving poor 12, 69; factors for poverty 68–70, 105; *see also* absolute poverty; historical reasons for reduction in poverty; international perspectives on poverty; in-work poverty; material deprivation; measuring poverty; monetary poverty; multidimensional poverty; persistent poverty; policies aimed at poverty; poverty development; quality of life and poverty; relative poverty; successful poverty reduction cases

poverty development: chapter overview 4–5, 35–36; decline in absolute poverty 36–37, **37**; in developed welfare states 35–36, 37, *38*, 39, **40**, 41–43; in developing countries 36, 43–48; summary 48

poverty gap: OECD definition *19*; OECD poverty gap figures (2017) 18, *20*, 21

poverty rates: OECD definition *19*; OECD poverty rates (in non-EU countries, 2014–16) 18, **19**

poverty reduction cases *see* successful poverty reduction cases

poverty trap 27–28, 57, 78

preventing poverty 70–72, 102

public sector spending on social policy, and relative poverty development 39

purchasing power parities (PPP), and relative poverty measurement 16–17

quality of life and poverty: chapter overview 5, 53–54; cross-cutting issues 54; happiness and poverty 62–63, **63**; in-work poverty 56–60, **59**; poverty impact on children 55–56, 57; poverty in old age 60–61; summary 63–64

redistribution 17, 28, 43, 69, 70, 77, 81

relative poverty: concept 4, 9–10, *12*; and developed countries 3, 10; development of in affluent welfare states 37, *38*, 39, **40**, 41–43; and economic/non-economic growth 71; measuring 16–21, 29–30; and number of children 55; OECD countries 18, 19, **19**, *20*, 21; purchasing power parities (PPP) 16–17; relative poverty line 16–17, 18; 'at risk' of poverty (EU) 16–18, **17**, **18**; and role of welfare state 17; and size/role of family 16

relative poverty position 10, 11, 27–28

remittances 94, 95–96, 99

rent controls 81

resources, rights to, and absolute poverty measurement 13

the rich, and inequality/injustice 29

robots 98, 99

Romania: 'at risk' of in-work poverty 59, **59**; 'at risk' of poverty **40**; net official development support as percentages of GDP (2017) *97*

Rowntree, B. Seebohm 12–13

rural poverty: China 45–46; India 46; Japan 46

Russia, net official development support as percentages of GDP (2017) *97*

Rwanda, happiness levels **63**

sanitation, access to and quality of life 62

Saunders, Peter 17, 80

self-employment, and in-work poverty 58

self-responsibility, and poverty 69

Sen, Amartya 10, 21, 28

Shemesh, Yhonatan 68

single parent households 56, 57, 69, 74, 75

Slovak Republic: 'at risk' of in-work poverty **59**; 'at risk' of poverty **40**; net official development support as percentages of GDP (2017) *97*; poverty gap *20*, 21

Slovenia: 'at risk' of in-work poverty **59**; 'at risk' of poverty **40**; net official development support as percentages of GDP (2017) *97*; poverty gap *20*, 21

social capital 54, 57, 71

social exclusion 26, *26*, 37, **40**

social indicator movement (1960s), having, loving and being indicators 11, **11**

social policy *see* policies aimed at poverty; welfare states

social protection: and economic growth 72; and ILO 91; *see also* benefits; welfare states

social security contributions, and reducing poverty 76, 77

Somalia, multidimensional poverty 24

South Africa, poverty gap *20*, 21

South America *see* Latin America

South Asia: absolute poverty statistics **15**, 16, 37, **37**; multidimensional poverty 24

South Sudan: absolute poverty 15; happiness levels **63**; multidimensional poverty 24

Spain: 'at risk' of in-work poverty **59**, 60; 'at risk' of poverty **40**; net official development support as percentages of GDP (2017) *97*; poverty gap *20*

state: role of in alleviating poverty 7; *see also* welfare states

Sub-Saharan Africa: absolute poverty 43, 44, 48, 105; absolute poverty statistics **15**, 16, 36, **37**; increase in population numbers and poverty 104; migration from 93; multidimensional poverty 24; poverty reduction problems 2, 4, 16, 30; and transfer of resources 104–105

successful poverty reduction cases 101–103, 105

Sudan *see* South Sudan

Sweden: 'at risk' of in-work poverty **59**; 'at risk' of poverty **40**; net official development support as percentages of GDP (2017) *97*; poverty gap *20*

Switzerland: net official development support as percentages of GDP (2017) *97*; old age poverty 60; poverty gap *20*; relative poverty rates 18, **19**

Tanzania, happiness levels **63**

tax credits 77–78, 81, 103

taxes: and reducing poverty 76–78, 81, 83; reduction of in return for helping people in need 81; value added taxes 77; *see also* redistribution

technology, and poverty 98, 99

Thailand, net official development support as percentages of GDP (2017) *97*

transfers from rich to poor countries *see* development support; remittances

transport, as in-kind benefit 75–76

Turkey: net official development support as percentages of GDP (2017) 96, *97*; poverty gap *20*; relative poverty rates 18, **19**

underclass 69
UNICEF: and multidimensional poverty 91; poverty data 43, 55
United Arab Emirates, net official development support as percentages of GDP (2017) 96, *97*
United Kingdom (UK): 'at risk' of in-work poverty **59**; 'at risk' of poverty **40**; first studies on poverty 4, 9, 12–13; migrant workers' impact on society 94; net official development support as percentages of GDP (2017) *97*; old age poverty 60; poverty gap *20*; relative poverty development 39; Voluntary Living Wage 81; *see also* England
United Nations (UN): goal of eradicating extreme poverty 1, 4, 6, 9, 30, 90, 104–105; goal of sustainable development 6; goals for development support 96
United Nations Convention on the Rights of the Child 55
United Nations Development Programme (UNDP) 90
United States (US): child poverty 41–42, 56; in-work poverty 58; in-kind benefits 42; migrant workers and risk of poverty 95; multidimensional poverty 42; net official development support as percentages of GDP (2017) *97*; poverty gap *20*; relative poverty development 37, 41–42, 48; relative poverty rates 18, **19**; welfare reform (1996) 41
Uruguay, poverty rates 47

value added taxes 77
Venezuela, conditional cash transfers (CCTs) 47
Vietnam, poverty reduction 46
Voluntary Living Wage (UK) 81

wages: migrant workers' impact on 94; minimum wage 57, 80–81, 95, 101–102; Voluntary Living Wage (UK) 81; wage subsidies 79; *see also* income; in-work poverty; labour market
wars/conflicts, and poverty 70, 103–104, 105
water, access to and quality of life 62
welfare states: and child maintenance support 56; financing of policies 72, 76–78; and in-work poverty 60; and measured vs perceived poverty 27; and measurement of absolute poverty 14; and measurement of relative poverty 17; and migrant workers 94–95; and old age poverty 60–61; poverty development in affluent welfare states 35–36, 37, *38*, 39, **40**, 41–43; and preventing poverty 70; and reduction in absolute poverty 37; and reduction in poverty 39, 42, 44, 48, 102–103, 104; US welfare reform (1996) 41; *see also* benefits; policies aimed at poverty; taxes
women: pensions 61; single women households 57; violence against 54; *see also* single parent households
working poor *see* in-work poverty
World Bank: about 92; absolute poverty definition 15; and conditional cash transfers (CCTs) 47; poverty data 43
World Food Programme 90
World Health Organization (WHO) 91